THE LUDLOW MASSACRE
of 1913-14

THE LUDLOW
MASSACRE
of 1913-14

Rosemary Laughlin

MORGAN
REYNOLDS
PUBLISHING
Greensboro, North Carolina

american workers

The Homestead Steel Strike of 1892

The Pullman Strike of 1894

The Ludlow Massacre of 1913-14

Mother Jones

THE LUDLOW MASSACRE OF 1913-14

Copyright © 2006 by Rosemary Laughlin

Library of Congress Cataloging-in-Publication Data

Laughlin, Rosemary.
    The Ludlow massacre of 1913-14 / Rosemary Laughlin.— 1st ed.
    p. cm.
    Includes bibliographical references and index.
    ISBN-13: 978-1-931798-86-0 (library binding)
    ISBN-10: 1-931798-86-9 (library binding)
    1. Coal Strike, Colo., 1913-1914—Juvenile literature. 2.
Massacres—Colorado—Ludlow—History—20th century—Juvenile literature.
I. Title.
    HD5325.M6161913 L38 2006
    331.892'8223340978896—dc22
                                        2005030050

Printed in the United States of America
First Edition

CONTENTS

Chapter One
The Strike Scene 9

Chapter Two
A Miner's Life 20

Chapter Three
The Rockefellers 33

Chapter Four
United Mine Workers 45

Chapter Five
Demands 61

Chapter Six
Voice of the Gun 71

Chapter Seven
Martial Law 83

Chapter Eight
War 98

Chapter Nine
Defeat 108

Chapter Ten
Consequences 120

Timeline 134
Sources 137
Bibliography 141
Web sites 142
Index 143

The Ludlow Massacre. (Library of Congress)

1.
The Strike Scene

September 23, 1913, the day the United Mine Workers had chosen as the first day of their strike against the Colorado Fuel and Iron Company (CFI), was an unseasonably nasty day on the eastern foothills of the Rocky Mountains. A north wind whipped rain and snow across the dirt streets and the wood and cement-block miners' cottages near Ludlow, Colorado. The company owned the houses, which meant that when the union miners stopped work they were forced out. Mine guards methodically checked each cottage and tossed belongings into the muddy streets. Families huddled together as they waited for wagons to transport them and their belongings to the makeshift tent cities that would be their homes over the long mountain winter. A reporter from a Denver newspaper,

The strike at Ludlow, which lasted from September 1913 to December 1914, forced the coal miners and their families to live in makeshift tent colonies through the harshest of Rocky Mountain weather. (Courtesy of the Denver Public Library, Western History Collection, X-60350.)

who watched the slowly moving lines of workers and their families leaving their homes, described the scene as "an exodus of woe . . . of a people born to suffering going forth to a new suffering."

The families walked out of coal camps all over the range. Many of the camps were built in canyons so narrow that they could only hold two or three rows of small houses. The women, children, and striking workers trudged along roads that led towards the vast Great Plains on the east:

Every wagon was the same with its high piled furniture, and its bewildered woebegone family perched atop. And the furniture! What a mockery to the state's boasted riches. Little piles of rickety chairs. Little piles of miserable looking straw bedding. Little piles of kitchen utensils. And all so worn and badly used they would have been the scorn of any second-hand dealer.

John Lawson, a big blond man dressed in rough woolen clothes and high-topped boots who was leading the strikers, had to find places for the 12,000 displaced people. He had set up tent homes provided by the United Mine Workers (UMW) union. These were the same kind of temporary housing the military used for soldiers. Wood floors were laid aboveground and wood walls added. A cooking stove was put in and central posts held up the tent roofs. Each of the dozen or more colonies had one large central tent to serve as a school and meeting hall.

On the morning of September 23, John Lawson was upset because one thousand tents sent from West Virginia had not arrived. Because of the missing tents, Lawson had no choice but to double up families or find lodging for them with sympathetic residents of nearby towns. The lack of tents and the bitter weather discouraged the drenched families. But their spirits and their support for the strike were not totally washed away. Lawson could occasionally hear singing coming from some of the wagons.

On that cold September day, as he listened to the singing and watched the families struggle into their new tent homes, John Lawson must have felt the weight of all of their dreams and fears on his shoulders. The strike against the coal companies of southern Colorado had been coming a long time. Over the years, the differences between the workers aided by the UMW, and the companies, particularly the huge CFI, had grown more marked. The UMW was determined to have an official say in how the mines were operated. The workers were convinced that their safety and well-being could only be protected by an organization of their peers who knew what they went through every day deep in the mines. On the other side, the companies were equally convinced that the American principles of private property and individual liberty protected them from having to recognize the union.

The Ludlow tent colony consisted of about two hundred tents holding 1,200 miners and their families, one of the largest of the UMW colonies. (Courtesy of the Denver Public Library, Western History Collection, X-60469.)

It was a long-brewing battle that had finally resulted in a strike. Both sides were determined to prevail. The stresses of the weeks and months ahead would be terrible, and the tragic consequences of the Colorado coalfield strike of 1913-1914 would resound for decades to come.

Coal, an important source of energy, is a natural product. Eons ago, plants and trees decayed and were submerged by water, then covered with rocks, minerals, and sediment. Over millions of years, these once-living organisms were pressured into a solid mineral called carbon. The process of pressuring dead vegetation into carbon sometimes involves earthquakes. Geologists have labeled the period when most of the world's coal was formed the Carboniferous period, which was approximately 280 million years ago. Additional coal formation, and much of the upheaval and separation that allows coal to be mined, occurred later, in the Mesozoic era, 65 to 225 million years ago.

The coal formation process happened all over the globe, but variations in that process resulted in different types of coal. At some point, it was discovered that coal could be burned and that it provided a long-lasting source of heat and light. Coal that has the greatest proportion of fixed carbon and the least amount of moisture provides a longer-lasting, more intense heat. By modern times, several other uses for coal had been developed.

The two basic categories of coal are bituminous and

After mining anthracite coal, workers had to use hammers to break it into smaller lumps. (Courtesy of the Granger Collection.)

anthracite, and each of these has different grades. Bituminous is deep black, does not crumble easily, and burns readily, though producing dirty smoke. Anthracite is lustrous black and very hard; it is nearly pure carbon and burns cleanly. It is the more desirable, for it pollutes the least.

During the Industrial Age of the 1800s, coal replaced wood as people's major source of energy. Woods and forests are limited to the surface of the earth, and growing, migrating populations were rapidly depleting them. Coal also produces heat more efficiently and burns longer than wood. Coal, therefore, became the major fuel for factories, railroads, and steamships. It heated people's homes and provided gas for the lights in cities and houses. By the end of the century, oil products began to compete with coal in some uses—kerosene-fueled lamps and grease eased the moving parts of machinery—but coal remained very important. When electricity began to transform life in the United States and other developed countries, coal was the primary fuel used to run the engines that generated electricity.

At the beginning of the twentieth century, coal fueled most steam locomotives and ships. Tar, the gummy oil in coal that was removed by crushing the coal, was the basic substance for products ranging from dyes, paints, and explosives to flavorings, perfumes, and drugs. Almost all homes and commercial buildings had coal furnaces; chutes for coal delivery to the basement were a standard feature. A low railroad car with unloading chutes in its bottom, called a coal hopper, carried the coal from the mines to major delivery points.

The industrialization that occurred in the United States after the Civil War was built on steel. It was used to make train rails, automobiles, bridges, cables, tall buildings, and countless other products of the industrial era.

The city of Pittsburgh, Pennsylvania, with its accessible location at the confluence of three rivers and its ready supply of coke-grade coal, became one of the hubs of steelmaking in the United States. Dozens of steel mills can be seen operating on the city's outskirts in this turn-of-the-century print. (Library of Congress)

Coal was essential for the production of steel. In Pittsburgh and other steelmaking centers, methods had been developed to remove the impurities from iron, which was the basic ingredient in steel. These processes required temperatures that only higher-grade coal could produce. Coke, which was made from high-grade bituminous coal, provided the fuel to heat the iron to such high temperatures.

It is easy to see why this fuel source was sometimes called "King Coal." Coalfields are spread throughout the United States. There are the Appalachian fields that stretch from Pennsylvania to Alabama; the eastern interior region of Illinois, Kentucky, and Indiana; the northern interior in Michigan; the western interior of Iowa, Kansas, Missouri, Oklahoma, and Arkansas; the Gulf

Coast of Texas and Louisiana; the Pacific fields in Washington state; and the huge Rocky Mountain coalfields of Colorado, Wyoming, Utah, New Mexico, Montana, and North Dakota.

Colorado's coalfields covered 25,000 square miles and equaled one quarter of the nation's eighth-largest state. Though this gave Colorado the distinction of having more bituminous coal than any other state, geologists found that half of it was buried too deeply for profitable mining. But there was plenty that could be dug up. During the nineteenth century, there were productive fields in three primary areas: the western slopes of the Continental Divide in the Rocky Mountains, and the northern and southern fields on the eastern side of the Divide.

By 1900, 60 percent of Colorado's coal output came from the southeastern area, between the towns of Walsenburg and Trinidad. This area was usually referred

This late-nineteenth-century lithograph gives a bird's-eye view of the CFI-controlled mining town of Trinidad, Colorado. (Library of Congress)

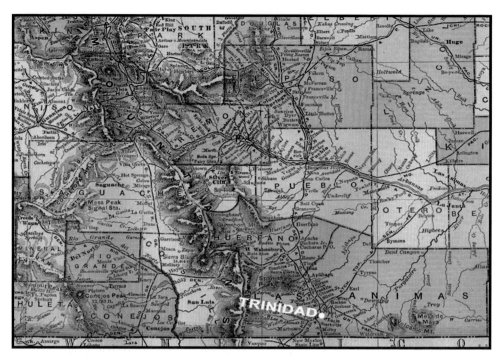

Trinidad sits in Las Animas County, just east of the Rocky Mountain range that bisects the state, and near Colorado's southern border with New Mexico. (Library of Congress)

to as the Trinidad field. It was about fifty miles long and varied from five to twenty miles wide. Las Animas and Huerfano counties were the richest of all for coking coal. The high-grade bituminous coal here boasted a rich blackness and a lustrous sheen, and broke into cube-like pieces. These mines were very accessible, located where the western end of the Great Plains met the foothills of the Rocky Mountains, and had become the chief source for coke west of the Mississippi River.

The coal was taken from the mine in railroad cars. The Atchison, Topeka & Santa Fe Railroad came in from Kansas to the east and continued south from Trinidad over Raton Pass into New Mexico. The Denver & Rio Grande, the Colorado & Southern, and the Colorado &

Wyoming Railroads also came to the fields. The railroads had been built in the 1870s and 1880s, during a period of discoveries of gold and silver that had ignited rushes to create mines. These rushes were soon past, but the railroads stayed on to serve the coal mines.

Colorado became a state in 1876, the same year its coal output surpassed 100,000 tons. Also in 1876, the Denver and Rio Grande Railroad founded the Colorado Coal and Iron Company. The new company then constructed the first big coke ovens in the state, near the town of El Moro, bringing steel and iron manufacturing to Colorado. This, in turn, increased the need for coal, and by 1882, the mined tons reached one million.

2.
A Miner's Life

The miner's day usually began and ended in darkness, and his job was both difficult and dangerous. Death and injury could come from many directions. Cave-ins, deadly gas leaks, explosions, and floods happened suddenly, with little warning.

Colorado coal was mined mostly by the room-and-pillar method. Rooms were dug out of a coal seam, a layer of coal between two layers of rock, and pillars were left to support the roof. Over time a subterranean mine would become a maze of connecting rooms and the occasional dead end.

After descending to the work level, the coal diggers walked through the main tunnels to a seam that had not yet been mined. They worked in pairs in dim lighting, surrounded by the thick underground darkness. The

Colorado coal miners labor in near darkness, repeatedly hammering an underground coal seam with their picks. (Library of Congress)

conditions were cramped. The diggers often swung their picks while kneeling or on their backs. They also drilled holes for the explosives used to loosen the coal. At any time they might encounter a fracture, an irregularity in the strata caused by the upheaval of the Rocky Mountains, which are, geologically, relatively young, and a sudden cave-in would crash the ceiling in around them. Another cause of sudden death or injury came when the drillers tapped into a gas pocket and released toxic fumes.

Black dust got into the miners' lungs and made them cough; eventually it resulted in the fatal black lung disease. Arthritis became the miner's constant companion, a result of working in uncomfortable positions in the damp underground.

There were other jobs necessary to get the coal out of the ground. Timbermen, who followed the diggers into freshly dug rooms, sawed logs used to help strengthen the doorways and roofs. Shot firers came in when the diggers and timbermen were gone to judge the right amount of powder and nitroglycerine to tamp into the drilled holes. They ignited the shot with a line connected to an electric battery. If all went well, coal would be loosened for the diggers to pick out in the morning; if not, the debris would have to be cleared away and the process redone.

Blacksmiths shod the mules that hauled coal to the main corridors, where electric trolley cars on tracks hauled it aboveground to be weighed. Electricians and pumpmen were on hand to keep the machinery in working order. They also kept the crucial air circulation fans working so miners would not suffocate.

These workers were all paid by the day, while digging miners were paid by the amount of coal they mined, or more specifically the tonnage of coal that could actually be sold. Digging miners had to separate the coal from the non-coal rock and clear away rock that might have been blasted by an overcharge of powder. Often, they had to help with propping up the timbers. These tasks were called "dead work" because the miners were not paid for it and could easily be dead if they skimped on doing it.

Aboveground, rail cars carried the good coal over a scale where it was weighed before being tipped, by means of a mechanical device called a tipple, into coal hoppers or storage piles. If the scale was not accurate, the miner would not receive the money he deserved for his hard work. This system was easily corrupted. A dishonest weighman could shift credit to himself or to a conspirator. These injustices frequently happened, and the miners often felt cheated and angry and wanted to have a weighman of their own choice at each tipple.

State inspectors often found errors of up to several hundred pounds in the scales. The deputies of the Colorado Mine Inspector, who were tasked with inspecting the scales, filed so many reports of short weight that the Colorado legislature passed a law allowing miners to elect their own weighman with access to the scales, tipple, and record books. Passing a law is one thing; enforcing it is another. The check-weighman law was not enforced in the Trinidad field, primarily because of intimidation. Miners were afraid they would lose their jobs if they complained, and those who asked to check the records were accused of not trusting their fellow miners. There were not enough state inspectors to check the mines, so mine operators were generally able to ignore the law.

Most of the coal diggers had no choice but to seethe

in silence. Another cause of resentment was the length of the workday. A 1902 amendment to the Colorado Constitution supposedly established an eight-hour day for all workers, but it was largely ignored by the mine operators. The miners worked for twelve or more hours a day if the demand for coal was there. If they refused to work long hours, their jobs would be given to other men who came west looking for work. The mine operators said that it was foolish for the men to reject the opportunity to work longer hours and dig more coal, which would earn them more money. What the managers chose to ignore was that the long hours increased the possibility that the tired men would make a mistake that could result in death or injury.

The pay rates of the Colorado miners were comparable to those of other American miners—the same or a little lower than wages of unionized miners in Wyoming, and a little higher than the wages in the unionized but more competitive mines of Kansas, Oklahoma, and Missouri. The Colorado operators hoped to discourage unionization by paying their men slightly more than unionized miners in other areas. The operators wanted to keep the unions out of their mines for fear they would lose control of their businesses.

In 1913, a Colorado miner averaged $3.50 a day in *gross wages* (before any deductions); that would equal about $62.66 in 2002. By comparison, a minimum-wage ($5.50 per hour) worker today would earn $44 in gross wages for an eight-hour shift. Of course, the miner might have worked more than eight hours for his daily average. However, there was more to the numbers than these figures suggest. Because coal demand was seasonal, mines operated between 175-200 days a year. In 1911, the fully employed miner averaged about $696 for the year. Charges for powder, blacksmithing, and medical treatment were deducted from their gross wages, as was $1 a month for the miner's family to be allowed to use the camp doctor or hospital. In 1912, the Colorado Bureau of Labor Statistics figured that coal miners averaged $1.68 a day in *net wages* (after all deductions), the equivalent of $31.16 in 2002.

Of course, working in a coal mine was considerably more dangerous than most of today's minimum-wage jobs. In 1913, a total of 110 men died in Colorado mines and another 354 were badly disabled. Mine operators usually attributed accidents to the carelessness of the miners. For example, records in Huerfano County for 1905-1914 describe ninety coroners' verdicts handed down on fatal mine accidents. Only one blames the mine operators. Typical phrases in the reports are "accident unavoidable," "death by neglect on his part and no other," "run over by a car due to negligence of the deceased," or "gross neglect in not timbering."

Operators found ways to enhance profits outside of the mines. The workers and their families, isolated in the small towns and camps, often had little choice but to buy their supplies at company-owned stores. If the camp was far from a town, where there were no other stores to

This 1873 engraving depicts the gruesome aftermath of one of the many coal-mine explosions that gave the profession its dangerous reputation. The confined underground environment often made accidents and explosions deadly, largely because of limited access for rescue operations. (Courtesy of the Granger Collection.)

compete with, the company stores sometimes raised their prices. CFI had a chain of stores that operated under the name Colorado Supply that made a 20 percent profit. In 1899, Colorado banned the use of "scrip" for miners' paychecks instead of U.S. money, but this law was also usually neglected. Scrip was good only at company stores. Saloons, too, were often owned by the company, and scrip made it easy for the men to buy drinks.

Fences completely enclosed many of the mining camps, and security guards controlled who came and went. The roads to the camps were also on company property. Some mine properties had incorporated towns within them. A few miners owned their own frame homes outside of the camps, and some immigrants were allowed to build shanties up in the canyons. Those who rented the company's wood-frame houses or concrete-block cottages at $2 per room, per month, gave the company a 6 to 8 percent profit. CFI's rent contracts stated that the company could give only three days' notice for the miner to evacuate the premises; if he did not comply, he would be "dispossessed" by having all his belongings removed.

Typical mining camp houses were small, simple frame structures built close together. This photograph shows the mining camp in Berwind, Colorado, located close to the Ludlow camp. (Courtesy of the Denver Public Library, Western History Collection, X-60377.)

The miners were vulnerable to abuse from a variety of people. The pit boss in the mine might tell a miner to buy insurance from him or lose his job. The store manager might threaten to get a miner fired if he did not buy at his store. Immigrant miners who spoke little English were the most vulnerable. They feared all supervisory and administrative people and usually did what they were told, regardless of rights they had under the law.

Mining camps did provide schools, though they were usually small and crowded, and a library, though it did not allow controversial books or magazines. Controversial meant any material presenting muckraking articles that exposed the injustices done to workers. *Harper's Weekly* was one such banished magazine. The Denver *Express,* a newspaper that favored unions, was also not allowed.

Sanitation in the mining towns and camps was usually rudimentary at best. The outdoor privies were primitive, and most of the camps got their water from the same reservoirs that received the runoff from the coal mines. Sometimes sewage from a town upstream would find its way downstream to the next town's drinking supply. In 1912, there were 157 cases of typhoid, which comes from polluted water, reported in CFI camps.

The situation was allowed to continue because of the operators' influence over politicians and government officials. Mine operators hired people to arrange precinct boundaries, fix nominations, intimidate voters, stuff ballot boxes, and bribe or intimidate judges and officials they did not "own." One attorney general described the system as a "very perfect political machine, just as much as Tammany in New York."

The man who most symbolized this political corruption was the sheriff of Huerfano County. Jefferson "King" Farr was a transplanted Texan who considered union organizers to be "agitators" and enemies of the county Republican Party. Farr owned cattle, property, and saloons in Huerfano County. He used his power and money supplied by CFI to control juries and the coroner, who were expected to render verdicts favorable to the coal operators—or else they lost their jobs.

In his saloons, Farr set up spies who eavesdropped on the workers' discussions. He also paid miners to give him information on union activities and to point out union men. Miners reported as complaining about conditions or speaking against the operators were accosted by mine guards or given "the kangaroo," a physical beating. If this pounding did not bring a miner into line, he would be sent "down the canyon." This meant he would be put on a freight train and dumped in the desert without food or water. If he returned, he ran the risk of being put on a blacklist of those who would not be hired by other operators. Sheriff Farr would even deputize mine guards so this treatment could be done under cover of the law.

A Colorado lawyer, Edward P. Costigan, tried to help reform the court practices in the Trinidad field counties. He questioned and criticized the labor practices of the mine operators and ran for office, though with little success, several times. He summed up the power of the coal companies as "ownership of courts, executive and legislative officials, of coroners' and other juries, of the churches, of the saloons, of the schools, of the lands, of the houses upon the lands, and eventually a certain ownership of the men who toil upon the lands."

Another factor that allowed the operators to maintain their control was the constant influx of immigrants from southern and eastern Europe—including Italy, Austria, Serbia, Croatia, Greece, Germany, Romania, Bulgaria, Hungary, Russia, and Poland—into the Colorado coal fields. Other immigrants came from Mexico and Japan. They all were seeking a better life in the United States, and they believed the glowing stories they heard from the brochures of railroads and steamship lines. When the European immigrants discovered that the East Coast labor force was saturated, they had little choice but to move westward.

The largest group of immigrants into the eastern slope of the Rockies was the Greeks. In 1907, Greece was devastated by a crop failure of currants used for wine, the base of its economy. From 1906-1914, an average of 31,000 men left Greece each year. Many ended up in Colorado, eager to work.

All the immigrants were exploitable labor. They spoke different languages and often had not yet learned to communicate in English. Their bosses further excercised control by separating workers who shared a common

A diverse group of young coal mine workers in 1911. (Library of Congress)

language. The men were often alone, homesick, bitter, and quarrelsome.

Even miners born in the United States, and those who could speak English, faced limited options—and they were not alone. Steel workers, lumber and construction men, farm workers, textile mill workers, and rubber and auto workers all faced huge challenges when they attempted to improve their safety, security, and pay. Organizing into a union often brought on strikes and abuse. In 1892, open warfare had broken out in Homestead, Pennsylvania, when steelworkers went out on strike; in 1911, dozens of workers, most of them women, had burned to death in the terrible fire at the Triangle

Shirtwaist factory in New York City. Since its inception, the United States had struggled to define the proper relationship between workers and those who profited from their labor. It was an issue that had motivated America's bloody Civil War, and continues to spark controversy today. The tragic events of 1913-1914 in the minefields of southern Colorado would be another terrible chapter in that ongoing conflict.

3.
The
Rockefellers

The Colorado coalfield owners shared a deep conviction with most other nineteenth-century capitalists that natural resources were there for the taking. The only barrier to profiting from coal, timber, oil, or other resources was the cost of getting it out of the ground. There was no justification to the idea that the resources belong to everyone and that the owners should have to pay a price for exploiting them. It was a race, from their perspective, that favored the fastest and the biggest operator.

The ends that justified their means were the concept of maximum profits and the owners' often-repeated obligation to provide profits to the stockholders. Profits for stockholders were valued far more than the concept of treating workers fairly. Their counter argument to those who insisted working conditions should be humane and that workers should share in the wealth by earning higher wages was to retort that workers were not slaves. They always had the right to quit and find other jobs if they did not like the salary or conditions offered by the employer. In this same vein, owners said that unions were villainous because they were organized to wrest control of private property from the owners. Private property and the rights that protected it were more important than the human rights of workers. Any philosophy based on assumptions of rights for the worker to be safe, fairly paid, and to negotiate his terms of employment was by definition evil because it limited the right of owners to do what they wished with their private property. They argued that wage and safety laws and regulations were not rights granted to workers but were illegal restraints of trade.

John C. Osgood believed the arguments put forth by the owners. Osgood was a bookkeeper from Ottumwa, Iowa, who carefully noted which accounts he worked on were profitable. Anxious to participate in the profits and not merely tabulate them for others, he bought into an Iowa coal-mining company and soon became its president. He also became affiliated with the Chicago, Burlington & Quincy Railroad, which had tracks to Denver. It was because of this connection that he first toured the Colorado coalfields.

By 1889, Osgood had organized the Colorado Fuel Company, which had mines on both the western and

Originally from Brooklyn, New York, John C. Osgood made his name as an industrialist and a proponent of the "model city" concept in Colorado. (Library of Congress)

eastern sides of the Rockies, including the rich field between Walsenburg and Trinidad. By 1890, he had plans for a steel works in Denver called Colorado Coal & Iron Company that would have the only blast furnace and converter, which used pressurized air to purify crude iron into steel, between the Missouri River and the Pacific Ocean. He would be able to supply the rails and wire fences needed in abundance as people poured into the vast expanses of the West. In 1892, he merged his two holdings into the Colorado Fuel & Iron Company, and by 1900, CFI owned mines in Wyoming and ran another steel plant in Pueblo, Colorado.

Early on Osgood realized that satisfied workmen were more productive and brought in higher profits. He called these "common-sense business ideas," and fostered them by creating a model town and setting up social programs in his other camps. He may have been inspired in part by the model town of railway car magnate George Pullman, founded in 1881 near Chicago. The aim was to unify pleasing homes, business, and public buildings with efficient power, sanitation, and transportation systems.

Redstone was Osgood's model town in the gorgeous Crystal River Valley of the Western Rockies, where he had a palatial home. Here he could feel like a parent who expected gratitude from his employee "children," an example of what came to be called industrial paternalism.

Osgood named his opulent forty-two-room mansion in Redstone "Cleveholm Manor," but the residence is now commonly referred to as "the Redstone Castle." By the time Cleveholm was completed in 1902, the estate included servants' quarters, a gamekeeper's lodge, a carriage house, and a greenhouse. (Courtesy of the Denver Public Library, Western History Collection, X-17787.)

Osgood's smaller camps often had the inferior housing and infrastructure of most of the mining camps in Colorado, but in the larger camps, Osgood's social programs included kindergartens, schools, night schools, lectures, libraries, musical societies, and parades on holidays such as the Fourth of July. He printed a company magazine with stories and pictures of happy miners and their families working and living at CFI.

In 1900, after Osgood had made CFI the strongest coal and steel company in the West, he began to deal and speculate with eastern financiers. In 1903, the fabulously wealthy oil titan John D. Rockefeller, always on the lookout for good investments, purchased 40 percent of CFI's stocks and 43 percent of its bonds. This essentially gave him controlling interest in CFI. It did not bother Rockefeller that Osgood had lost money by starting a plant he could not finish and did not even have enough cash to pay his workers. In order to gain control, Rockefeller quickly paid off the debts.

Rockefeller's control at CFI did not make the miners' lives better. Rockefeller was fiercely antiunion and believed in the primacy of profit. If a miner did not like working conditions, he was always free to go elsewhere.

Rockefeller and his son, John D. Rockefeller Jr., chose a man they trusted to help manage CFI as executive vice president and chief liaison to the Rockefeller staff in New York City. LaMont Bowers had won their respect when he designed and successfully ran a fleet of ships for carrying family-owned iron ore on the Great

John Davison Rockefeller, American capitalist and founder of the Standard Oil Company. (Library of Congress)

Lakes. Bowers seemed to be perfect for CFI. The Rockefellers had no intention of moving to Colorado, and Bowers wanted to move to the West.

By the turn of the twentieth century, John D.

Rockefeller had become the crowning symbol of everything that was both good and bad about American capitalism. Born in 1839, he was a self-made man. Gifted
with an intelligence ready-made for business, and armed
with self-discipline, a willingness to take huge but cal-
culated risks, an instinct for efficiency, and the drive to
work long and hard, he had accumulated the world's
largest personal fortune by middle age. Already in business in his native Cleveland as a merchant when oil was
discovered in large quantities in Pennsylvania, young
Rockefeller quickly turned a small investment into a
refinery and subsequently into Standard Oil, which at
one time controlled over 90 percent of the nation's oil
refineries. He bought oil fields to supply his refineries
with raw product, as well as railroads to transport the
oil, barrel plants to store it, research labs to develop
more uses for it, and outlets to retail kerosene and, later,
gasoline directly to the consumer. He, along with An-
drew Carnegie in the steel industry, perfected this ver-
tically integrated, self-contained form of corporation.

Rockefeller and his wife, Cettie, had four children,
whom they raised in a devoutly Baptist home. Rockefeller
led prayers and read the Bible daily. Cettie taught the
children at home and showed them that the most important values were their personal morality and relationship
with God. She taught them how to examine their con-
sciences each day and ask God's forgiveness for any
offenses.

Their only son, John Jr. (1874-1960), was a gentle,

sensitive boy who wanted to please both God and his parents. On the secular side, Junior and his sisters were trained to learn the value of money. They had to earn their spending money by doing chores, such as cutting brush, weeding, or mending broken pottery. They had to keep a record of all expenditures, which they regularly showed to their parents.

Oddly, Rockefeller Sr. did little to familiarize Junior with the companies he would one day be expected to run. He did not take him to visit the Standard Oil headquarters at 26 Broadway in New York City. Instead, the tycoon spent his time with the children playing games and enjoying outdoor sports, such as ice skating and horseback riding. He was an affectionate and kind father.

At home, Junior had only a few playmates. At twelve, he was sent to a school in New York City, where he was an excellent student and so conscientious that he exhausted himself from studying. After a few months of recovery doing outdoor work at the family's Cleveland estate, Junior finished high school and went on to college at Brown in Providence, Rhode Island. Brown was a Baptist school, and Junior loved his time there, where he was exposed to new ideas and experiences. While there he fell in love with Abby Aldrich, the daughter of the powerful U.S. senator from Rhode Island. She had a lively intelligence, a kind personality, and she loved the arts. She made a perfect wife for Junior, who adored her during their long, happy marriage. They would have six children, including Nelson, who would eventually

John Davison Rockefeller Jr. (Library of Congress)

become a governor of New York and vice president of the United States.

When Junior graduated from Brown in 1897, it was

time for him to go to work for his father, but he was self-consciously awkward and felt unprepared. He had always deferred to his father, of whom he was in awe his entire life.

When Junior entered the business, his father had recently retired from day-to-day operations. He no longer went to 26 Broadway each day and had left his vice president, John D. Archbold, in charge. But his lawyers and executives still briefed him and took his advice on business matters.

When he joined the firm, the quiet and reserved Junior was placed on the board of directors of Standard Oil and other Rockefeller companies. He was also on the board of the philanthropic Rockefeller Foundation, which his father had created in 1913 to encourage "the well-being of mankind throughout the world." From his earliest years, Senior believed firmly in his obligation to show thanks to God by donating to charities. After his retirement, he spent most of his time engrossed in giving money away.

The specific goals of the Rockefeller Foundation were to serve the public health, to give to institutions and programs that solved problems at their roots (for example, schools and colleges that prepared students for jobs, not systems to dole out money to jobless people), and to involve other donors through matching grants.

Junior loved the work the Rockefeller Foundation was doing. He saw the good it did at Spelman College, the University of Chicago, the Rockefeller Institute for

Medical Research, and the General Education Board. In fact, Junior never warmed to business and wanted to direct his full attention to the foundation. In 1910, he finally resigned from all the company boards, except one—Colorado Fuel and Iron.

Junior stayed on the CFI board because it was not as profitable as the other Rockefeller enterprises. He hoped that if he could make the company profitable, he might be worthy of his legendary father. He trusted LaMont Bowers to turn the company around and continued to rely on Bowers's operational control. A major management principle of both Rockefellers was to allow the managers on location to make decisions without daily interference from them. Their goal was long-term success, which they could oversee by going over the company's books in New York. This policy of placing capable men in powerful positions and allowing them to manage without hindrance—as long as the numbers were good—had served the family well for nearly fifty years. Neither of the Rockefeller men saw any reason to alter this strategy with CFI.

Junior was still learning about how CFI operated when the miners' long-stewing troubles came to a boil in 1912. His reflexive response was to believe what Bowers and CFI president Jesse Welborn told him about the situation in Colorado. They, of course, put the best face on events to show their authority and control. However, they themselves were located in Denver, miles away from the actual mines, and accepted their field superintendents' reports, as filtered for them by a regional manager in Pueblo. Each man in the chain naturally tended to report to his superior what he thought the superior wanted to hear.

Junior knew his father's hatred of labor unions. The self-made Senior saw unions as the first step in a long-term strategy on the part of progressive reformers, Socialists, and Communists to destroy capitalism and private enterprise. He had no intention of being the first domino to fall. If the mighty Rockefeller gave in to a union, what would stop all the other weaker companies from being taken over? He argued that the laboring class would abuse higher wages by spending them on useless or sinful activities—gambling, drinking, dancing, or going to shows and movies. He summarized his position by saying, "Soon the real object of their organizing shows itself—to do as little as possible for the greatest possible pay."

4.
United Mine Workers

By the time of the Civil War (1861-65) there were over twenty large unions in the United States. These early unions represented tradesmen and skilled laborers, such as printers, machinists, stonecutters, blacksmiths and locomotive engineers. Their goals were to obtain better pay and safe, humane working conditions.

A strike occurs when employees refuse to work as a way to force concessions from their employer. The earliest known strike in the U.S. was by printers in Philadelphia in 1786. From the beginning, strikers had to contend with the legal system as well as their employers, who had more influence over local, state, and federal governments. In 1806, Philadelphia cordwainers—leather workers, especially shoemakers—were the first to be convicted of criminal conspiracy for their strike. They would not be the last strikers to find themselves suddenly on the wrong side of the law.

Strikes became more frequent in the middle and late 1800s as waves of immigrants provided cheap labor that drove down wages and workers chafed at conditions that kept them near poverty. As industrialization increased after the Civil War, and more people left farms and small towns to work in the large new factories and mills, the frequency and intensity of strikes escalated. Among the major nineteenth-century strikes, which were usually over wage and job cuts, were the railroad uprisings of 1877, which involved train workers on the Baltimore & Ohio and other railroads mostly east of the Mississippi River; the Homestead Strike of steel workers against the giant Carnegie Steel Company in 1892; and the Pullman Strike of 1894, which pitted railway car makers against George Pullman in Illinois. Strikes continued in the new century. The anthracite coal strike of 1902, in Pennsylvania, had as its goal better wages, an eight-hour day, and safer conditions. President Theodore Roosevelt forced the mine operators into arbitration during this strike by leaking his plan to take over the mines and use federal troops to keep order if owners refused to negotiate with the workers.

American strikes have usually been violent. Striking workers would try to intimidate their replacements, and management would hire security guards, usually thugs, and battles often resulted. To restore order, and under pressure from powerful interests, a state governor could call out the militia, which usually ended up attacking the strikers. Political connections often made it easy for a wealthy employer to get the governor involved, which meant the strike would be handled at public expense. In the B&O strike and the Pullman Strike, federal troops became involved on the grounds that the strike was interfering with interstate commerce and the delivery of mail. Under this cover, President Grover Cleveland used federal troops to end the strikes and to prosecute union leaders. In the Pullman Strike, as in most others, unions were usually blamed for the bloodshed and inconvenience to the public.

By the second decade of the twentieth century, however, the political climate was changing, if only slightly. The Progressive Movement, which had slowly gained steam over the previous decades until it influenced the administration of Theodore Roosevelt, had been instrumental in the election of Woodrow Wilson in 1912. As more people were forced into factory jobs, and as journalists wrote of the terrible conditions of the new economy, the popularity of progressivism had grown. It was not as simple as it had once been for owners to accuse all union members of being political radicals who wanted to destroy the free market system. Roosevelt had talked about a "square deal" for all Americans, and finally, it was becoming an idea that could not easily be denied. Slowly, laws were being passed to solidify workers' rights. Concessions included laws regulating child labor and establishing limits for work hours per day.

Many of the gains made by workers were achieved or protected by unions. In 1869, a national organization called the Knights of Labor was founded to unite unions of industrial workers. Its motto was "An injury to one is the concern of all." It had some success in a strike against the Wabash Railroad in 1885. A year later, it lost prestige after losing the Missouri Pacific Railroad strike. But the biggest blow came from its association with the Haymarket Square riot in Chicago, during which seven policeman and four others were killed during a strike. The resulting bad publicity created a backlash against unions in general and the Knights of Labor specifically.

The Haymarket riot erupted in 1886 when workers at the Cyrus McCormick reaper plant in Chicago organized a strike around demands for an eight-hour workday. (Library of Congress)

Many workers switched their allegiance to the new American Federation of Labor (AFL).

During this chaos in the labor movement, miners went their own way and formed the United Mine Workers of America (UMW) in 1890. The UMW met with intense resistance from coal-mine operators, who complained that the UMW did not keep its contracts, decreased the efficiency and output of the mines, and thereby increased accidents. Despite this concerted resistance, the union grew. Initially, its largest gains were in the East.

A union called the Western Federation of Miners (WFM) began in Montana in 1893. Its basic goals were no different from those of the UMW, but its leaders were more radical and were willing to tolerate more violence against both the mines and strikebreakers (men brought in by the operators to replace striking workers), often derisively called scabs. At Cripple Creek, Colorado, in 1893, strikers attacked two gold mines before the militia was called in to restore order.

To counter the WFM, western mine owners formed the Mineowners' Association. The operators particularly hated the union's motto: "Labor produces all wealth; wealth belongs to the producer thereof." The Mineowners' Association tried to convince local sheriffs to deputize mine guards, which would allow them to use force against strikers. When the sheriffs refused, the owners would bargain with various governors and offer to pay the cost of calling out the militia if the governor would agree to order it during a strike.

Between 1903 and 1910, the WFM and the UMW supported several strikes. The operators used the press, which was usually on their side, to fight the unions. The WFM was blamed for railway explosions that killed more than twenty-five nonunion miners during one strike, although most of the bombs had been set by saboteurs hired by private security services, such as the Baldwin-Felts Detective Agency, with the goal of discrediting the strike. But the ploy worked, and when sheriffs asked the Colorado governor for help from the militia, the militia was called out and the strikes soon ended.

The miners in northern Colorado were mostly born in the United States and spoke English. They owned their own homes in nearby towns. This homogeneity of language and culture brought unity and strength to their chapters of the UMW. In a 1903-1904 strike, they were able to win higher pay. In 1908, they won the promise of an eight-hour day, paydays twice a month, pay for dead work, and increased safety measures.

The situation in the fields in southern Colorado was different. There, operators had shrewdly hired immigrants who did not speak English and often did not share a language. In 1912, the miners in the Trinidad fields represented thirty-two nationalities and twenty-seven languages. They were virtually sealed into a system of dependence on a small number of fellow countrymen.

Their gains in the northern Colorado mines encouraged the officers of the UMW, who worked out of a headquarters in Indianapolis. Another encouraging sign was the election of a union-supported Democratic governor in 1908. The UMW decided to try to organize the southern Colorado coal miners.

Early in 1913, twenty-one pairs of UMW organizers were trained in Denver. Their task was to organize the miners at the CFI mines located between Walsenburg and Trinidad, Colorado. The UMW organizers were trained to deal with the mine operators and their private bodyguards and gun men hired from the Baldwin-Felts Detective Agency. Baldwin-Felts was one of the agencies, similar to the legendary Pinkerton Detective Agency, that had been created to provide strikebreakers and other security services to owners who wanted to break up unions and end strikes.

The UMW's organizing method was fairly dangerous and depended on coolness and acting skill. The men worked in pairs. One presented himself openly as an active union organizer. The passive partner came in as a miner looking for work, pretending to be antiunion, cursing unions and their leadership. His goal was to get close to the foreman or other boss. Once their confidence had been gained, the secret union organizer would create distrust by claiming that some of the men, who in reality were against the union, were undercover union men. If the organizer did his job well, these men, despite their protests, would be given the "kangaroo" and "run down the canyon" by the Baldwin-Felts guards, and union men would then be on hand to apply for their jobs.

This role required acting skill and the intelligence to carry off a dangerous subterfuge. However, despite its risks, the strategy was largely successful. At one point, 3,000 miners joined the UMW in one month.

The UMW in Colorado was lucky to have John Lawson as one of its leaders at this critical time. Lawson (1871-1945) was born in Pennsylvania to immigrants from Scotland. His father was a coal miner, and Lawson began mine work at age eight as a breaker boy. He sat, legs apart, in a box above a conveyor belt as coal moved beneath him. His job was to snatch the slate and rock from the coal and toss it aside. His arms were in constant motion. Gloves did not last, and his hands were always cut and bruised. Breaker boys learned to urinate on their hands to make them heal more quickly.

Lawson moved on to fanning air into the mines and, finally, at thirteen, to driving the mules hauling coal cars. His father belonged to the Knights of Labor, and Lawson was a union man from the beginning. He was also highly intelligent and had a thirst for learning. He took correspondence courses from the Scranton School of Mines. When his father got the chance to manage a mine in Oregon, Lawson went with him. The mine failed. When father and son went to western Colorado, they found work digging for CFI.

In Colorado, Lawson married a local rancher's daughter, who accepted her husband's dedication to the union and lived with his willingness to run the risks entailed by union organizing. A big man with blue eyes and a

United Mine Workers organizer John Lawson. (Library of Congress)

square jaw, Lawson was physically impressive and earned a reputation as a successful amateur prizefighter. He was not easily intimidated.

During the unsuccessful strike of 1903, Lawson's home was dynamited along with those of several other strikers. Lawson's wife, Olive, and their baby daughter, Fern, were home but survived. The suspected dynamiter was Perry Coryell, the owner of a small mine and a newspaper. Coryell was never tried for the crime, despite repeated investigations.

Lawson tried to return to the mines, but each mine he worked at was sabotaged. When Lawson moved to Nevada in search of work, Coryell declared in his newspaper that he had driven Lawson from the state. Lawson returned to show him it was not so. Coryell found him in a barbershop and shot the unarmed Lawson, crippling him for months.

When the story was reported in newspapers around the country, Lawson became known and admired everywhere. Coryell left the state. Lawson stayed and resolved to continue as a union organizer.

In 1907, Lawson began to dedicate all his energy to the UMW but soon found himself in a discouraging situation. Membership had dropped, morale was low, and UMW officers on the national level were squabbling to the point of weakening the union. Nevertheless, Lawson went on assignment to the northern Colorado mines where, largely because of his leadership, the miners won a major contract with seventeen mine operators the next year.

Lawson was now ready to take on the much more difficult Trinidad field in Huerfano and Las Animas counties in southern Colorado. Up to now, organizing there had relied on stealth. Organizers had hidden in the hills by day and snuck into the camps at night, careful to avoid the Baldwin-Felts guards. When he arrived in the area, Lawson knew he was no longer in Boulder County, where Sheriff MP Capp was honest and would not deputize the Baldwins. In contrast, Sheriff Farr of Huerfano County was in the pocket of the mine operators and was notorious for deputizing Baldwin agents and working with them.

By 1912, tensions in the Trinidad fields were at a breaking point. LaMont Bowers and CFI president Jesse Welborn were worried about the union's success in organizing the workers. They wanted to avoid a strike. Hoping to weaken the union and stave off more demands, they announced a 10 percent wage increase. Then, early in 1913, they granted payday twice a month and abolished scrip. In March, they reduced the work day to eight hours. They informed the miners that the changes were "not influenced in any way by the activities of union organizers."

Many of the miners, however, encouraged by the union organizers, were convinced that these improvements were being made now because of the union. Furthermore, the abolishment of scrip and many of the new safety measures were already Colorado law, but Bowers and Welborn acted as though these things had been granted by an act of benevolence on their part. Perhaps most important, the changes created a hope in the miners' minds and probably motivated them to work harder for their ultimate goal. That goal, as stated by

Lawson and the other officers of UMW's Colorado District 15 union, was to establish the right to organize into a union and as a union bargain with the mine operators for a contract.

During the 1913-14 strike, Lawson and the UMW were helped by the presence of the legendary Mary Harris Jones, better known as Mother Jones. Mother Jones has been described as a fiery revivalist preacher whose religion was unionism. She was called a rabble-rouser, an agitator, a witch, a woman of ill repute, and other denigrating names by mine operators. The miners, in contrast, saw her as "Joan of Arc disguised as a kindly old Irish grandmother." She seemed to be always on the spot when a strike loomed or an ongoing effort needed encouragement.

When asked where she lived, she snapped, "Wherever there is a fight." When once introduced as "a great humanitarian," she interrupted, "Get it right. I'm not a humanitarian; I'm a hell-raiser." Another progressive reformer, Daisy Harriman, agreed, saying Jones was "a fire-brand, foul-mouthed and partisan, a camp-follower and a comforter in the industrial war."

Mary Jones was born in Ireland sometime between 1830 and 1843. As a child, she came to America with her family and then moved to Canada, where her father worked building railroads. Mary went to a teacher's college in Toronto and then got a job in Michigan. She later went into dressmaking in Chicago before moving

Labor and community organizer Mary Harris "Mother" Jones worked until her death in 1930 to advocate for the rights of unions. She is known to this day as the Grandmother of All Agitators. (Library of Congress)

to Memphis, Tennessee, where she met her husband, George Jones, an iron moulder active in his trade union. Mary and George had several children.

Tragedy struck in 1867 when her husband and children all died during a yellow-fever epidemic. Jones returned to Chicago and worked successfully as a dressmaker. But when her building was destroyed by the Chicago fire of 1871, she was left homeless and penniless. With all her possessions gone, she lived for a time in a church.

As she attempted to reestablish her business, Jones listened to lectures by the Knights of Labor and became committed to the labor movement. By the 1890s, she was running a Socialist-labor newspaper in Kansas City. While on a trip to the Pennsylvania coal mines, she decided to join the UMW as a paid organizer. At first, the idea of a woman organizer of coal miners seemed like a lark to the mine owners, who thought she was a harmless crackpot. They soon found out otherwise.

Jones wisely cultivated her image as a "mother" to the miners and their families. This matronly appeal, combined with her zeal to better their lives, made her a beloved and influential figure. Jones saw life as a constant struggle between the classes. She wanted laborers to win control of the means of production and distribution in order to enhance their economic power. She did not hesitate to criticize those within the labor movement she thought were not honest or as dedicated as she was. When she thought UMW officers were acting like greedy capitalists in their style of living, she scolded them publicly. She got away with her criticism because she was so popular with the miners.

The UMW officers learned to let her do what she wanted. For example, she was involved with the founding of the International Workers of the World (IWW) in 1905, which aimed to put all workers in one union regardless of skill or industry. The UMW did not support the IWW, nor did the American Federation of Labor.

Mother Jones carried one little carpetbag with her and was always prepared to go to jail if arrested. Though she was middle-aged by the time she became a UMW organizer, her energy was boundless and her voice was like a bullhorn. She taunted mine guards to shoot an old lady. She feared nothing.

A reporter from the *Boston Herald* captured her flavor in this excerpt from a speech she gave to West Virginia miners in 1904:

> "Has anyone ever told you, my children, about the lives you are living here, so that you may understand how it is you pass your days on earth? Have you told each other about it and thought it over among yourselves, so that you might imagine a brighter day and begin to bring it to pass? If no one has done so I will do it for you today. . . ."

The writer then described Jones:

> So the old lady, standing very quietly, in her deep, far-reaching voice, painted a picture of the life of a miner from his young boyhood to his old age. . . . She talked of the first introduction a boy had to those dismal caves under the earth, dripping with moisture, often so low that he must crawl into the coal veins, must lie on his back to work. She told how miners stood bent over until the back ached too much to straighten, or in sulphur water that ate through the shoes and made sores on the flesh; how their hands became cracked and their nails broken off in the quick; how the bit of bacon and beans in the dinner pail failed to stop the craving of their

empty stomachs, and the thought of barefoot children at home and the sick mother was all too dreary to make the home-going a cheerful one.

"You pity yourselves, but you do not pity your brothers, or you would stand together to help one another," said Mother Jones. And then in an impassioned vein she called upon them to awaken their minds so that they might live another life. As she ceased speaking, men and women looked at each other with shamed faces, for almost every one had been weeping.

5.

Demands

In 1861, in his first annual message to Congress, President Abraham Lincoln spoke about the role of labor in an economy that had slaves as well as wealthy industrialists. His remarks captured the on-going tension between labor and capital. "Labor is prior to, and independent of, capital," he said. "Capital is only the fruit of labor, and could never have existed if labor had not first existed. Labor is the superior of capital and deserves much the higher consideration. Capital has its rights, which are as worthy of protection as any other rights."

In Colorado in 1913, critical unanswered questions hung over labor and capital. Would the labor movement be dominated by the moderate trade and industrial philosophy of unions such as the American Federation of Labor and the United Mine Workers? Or the radical unionists of the International Workers of the World? The management of CFI and the operators of the other Trinidad field coal mines expected continued government support for their right to free trade without the restraints of organized labor. But the recent settlement of strikes at eastern mines, and even in northern Colorado in 1908, made them uneasy.

During the summer of 1913, while union organizers infiltrated the ranks of the miners and recruited new members, a single policy committee was empowered by the UMW officers in Indianapolis to plot strategy, bargain, and give commands. John Lawson, Ed Doyle, and John McLennan of District 15, located in Colorado and New Mexico, were teamed with the UMW vice-president Frank J. Hayes, a former Iowa miner and West Virginia union organizer. They distributed an emotional invitation to the miners:

> This is the day of your emancipation. This is the day when liberty and progress come to abide in your midst. We call upon you this day to enroll as a member of the greatest and most powerful labor organization in the world, the United Mine Workers of America.

The letter assured the men of support if they joined the union and decided to strike: "If you are discharged for exercising your legal rights, we will begin court proceedings against the offending company and will

This membership certificate to the United Mine Workers outlines the union's goals in the preamble and shows an illustrated history of coal miners' arduous lot. (Library of Congress)

pay your strike benefits from the moment you quit work." The phrase "legal rights" referred to Colorado laws that prohibited corporations from interfering with their employees' organizations and to the "due process" guaranteed by the U.S. Constitution for any arrested person.

These were promises that had to be backed up. A Colorado lawyer, Horace Hawkins, was designated as counsel for the UMW in Colorado. The UMW national officers set aside a total of $1 million to fund weekly allowances for strikers: $3 for each worker, plus an extra $1 if he was married, and fifty cents for each child. This money came from the dues of UMW members, supplemented by a $1 strike-support assessment collected from nearly 400,000 members. The officers said they could probably provide $250,000 for each additional month if the $1 million ran out, which they did not expect to happen.

Over 9,000 Trinidad field miners joined the UMW. Most worked for CFI. About 2,000 miners in the northern fields also joined. Many were men who had taken the place of other miners during the 1903-04 strike; now they had similar problems.

Before going out on strike, the UMW set out its demands for CFI. There were seven:

1. Recognition of the union's right to bargain
2. A 10% advance in wages on tonnage rates
3. An eight-hour workday for all laborers in and

around mines and at coke ovens
4. Pay for dead work (timbering, brushing,
   removing rocks, handling impurities, etc.)
5. A check-weighman at all mines elected by the
   miners without interference
6. The right to trade in any store and to choose
   lodging and medical doctor
7. Enforcement of Colorado mining laws and
   elimination of armed mine guards

Demands 3, 5, 7, and parts of 6 were already protected by Colorado law. The UMW listed them because they had been ignored by managers and bosses at the mines. The financial demands in 2 and 4 were important, but all understood that the first demand was the most crucial. If the union was recognized as the legal representation of its members, the managers and owners could not decide to ignore the union during future negotiations. The leaders of the UMW and most of its members were determined to get legal standing for the union. They knew only a union would be able to advocate for fair wages and safer working conditions. They felt they deserved to be represented by an advocate, just as their employers had the right to hire lawyers to represent their interests.

The strike was not just against CFI. Among the mine operators who received the demands were some small mine owners and the "big three," who produced 75 percent of the Trinidad fields output: CFI, Rocky Mountain Fuel, and Victor-American Fuel. CFI was the largest of these. It produced 40 percent of the coal mined and employed the same proportion of workers. CFI also ran the steel mill that required a steady supply of coking coal. This put CFI at a greater risk. Not only did they need the coal, corporate officers were afraid that reaching a deal with the UMW would encourage the workers at the steel mill to organize and strike.

Governor Elias Ammons of Colorado, who had been elected in 1912, was very worried about a strike. He had come from poverty and, as a boy, worked odd jobs, such as cutting wood and lighting street gaslights, to help support his family. His eyesight had been weakened by the measles, but he still managed some schooling and

Colorado governor Elias Milton Ammons sits at his desk in 1913. (Courtesy of the Denver Public Library, Western History Collection, Z-8805.)

had gone into newspaper reporting, eventually becoming an associate editor of the *Denver Times*. When his eyesight grew worse, he became a rancher. Soon he was active in community service and politics and was elected a state legislator in 1890. He wanted peaceful prosperity and justice in his state.

Ammons knew that previous governors had sent in the militia during labor-management conflicts, and he still had vivid memories of 1904, when boxcars loaded with strikers were driven off and abandoned on the plains of Kansas, Texas, and New Mexico. Ammons did not want to have to call in the militia to break up another strike. He urged the mine operators to meet with the UMW and negotiate.

The operators of the Trinidad field mines refused to meet with the UMW. To do so would acknowledge the union's right to speak for their employees. They pointed out that they had already granted some of the demands; in effect, they were claiming that laws they had to obey, such as the eight-hour-day law, were actually concessions the companies had made.

The governor then sent state labor commissioner Edwin Brake to Trinidad to report on the situation and talk to the workers. Several of the miners were invited to participate in a State Federation of Labor conference to be held there on August 17, 1913.

Commissioner Brake arrived in Trinidad on August 15. As he checked in at the Toltec Hotel, he heard gunshots. He rushed outside to see Gerald Lippiatt, a northern

Baldwin-Felts agents were hired around the country to investigate train robberies and track down various criminals, but the detective agency became best known for its willingness to break labor strikes. (Library of Congress)

Colorado miner who had come to Trinidad to organize for the UMW, lying dead on the street. Lippiatt had run into George Belcher and Walter Belk, two agents from the Baldwin-Felts Detective Agency, and been shot dead.

Lippiatt had a limp, and when he passed by Belk and Belcher in the street, they bumped him with their elbows and cursed him. He cursed back. Angry, Lippiatt made the fatal error of going to his room to get his pistol. When he returned, armed, he dared Belk to repeat his remarks. "All right, you rat, let's have it out!" Lippiatt cried. Belk and Belcher drew their guns and shot Lippiatt at least eight times. Lippiatt fired once before he died, hitting Belk in the thigh.

After the shooting, the miners were furious. They did not see it as a kind of duel that Lippiatt had chosen, but as murder. A crowd gathered and Commissioner Brake became alarmed. But McLennan and several other organizers managed to get the men into the union headquarters and quiet them down.

The next morning the 150 delegates to the conference put on black mourning bands and draped Lippiatt's chair in black at the opening meeting. The governor had hoped the conference would show the way to reconciliation, but the shooting of Lippiatt ended any chance of that. The conferees pledged the support of labor throughout the state to the UMW and the miners.

A coroner's jury later pronounced the shooting justifiable homicide.

Brake returned to Denver and reported to Governor Ammons of "a terrible unrest" intensified by the Lippiatt killing. He advised the governor to declare martial law and to order the sheriffs of Las Animas and Huerfano counties to disarm every miner, mine guard, and detective. He did not seem to realize that the sheriff had already deputized many mine guards and detectives. To disarm the miners would leave them defenseless. At any rate, the governor did not take his advice.

One month later, on September 15, 1913, miners were invited to attend a meeting called by the UMW policy committee at the Toltec Hotel in Trinidad. For two days the leadership committee, chaired by John Lawson, listened to grievances. The complaints were familiar despite laws that had been passed that were intended to prevent them. Miners complained of bad scales that cheated them four hundred to eight hundred pounds on a carload of coal; payment in scrip worth only ninety cents on the dollar and usable only at company stores; being forced to vote as their superintendent told them; getting "kangarooed" for joining the unions; and being "sent down the canyon" for requesting a check-weigh-man chosen by a free election.

Mother Jones delivered her typical "give 'em hell" speech. A vote to strike was unanimously made, with a seven-day grace period for the operators to change their minds and meet with the union to negotiate. If the owners refused, the strike would begin on September 23, 1913.

Earlier in the summer, Ed Doyle and John Lawson had planned the physical details for the anticipated strike. They prepared housing for the families that would be evicted from company property. Doyle rented land near the mouths of the coal canyons, both to make the trip short and to make it easy to harass scabs—replacement workers—who came in to take the strikers' jobs.

Tent colonies were erected near Walsenburg, Rugby, Aguilar, Forbes, Suffield, and Sopris. The largest, located by the railroad spur leading to CFI's best mines, was a forty-acre area for 1,200 residents near the town of Ludlow. Foundations and walls were built, and tent ceilings were added when they arrived from UMW storage. The miners were prepared to dig in for what was expected to be a long fight.

6.

Voice of the Gun

The coal operators did not respond to the union's demands during the week given them. The U.S. labor secretary of the new administration of President Woodrow Wilson sent a representative to John D. Rockefeller Jr. at 26 Broadway in New York City, begging him to prevent the strike. Rockefeller refused to meet with him. Instead, he responded through his lawyer that the CFI managers in Colorado were entrusted to handle all management decisions and that they had reported they had the situation under control.

The strike began on an unseasonably wet and cold September 23, 1913. By September 27, the missing one thousand tents from West Virginia had arrived, along with better weather. Soon the majestic snow-tipped Rockies were looking down on tidy tent colonies organized around baseball diamonds and central meeting tents. Communication lines were established to the union headquarters in Trinidad. Lawson organized police volunteers to keep order, and he saw that committees were elected to keep up sanitation, communication, and entertainment.

In the beginning, morale was kept up by the efforts of several of the miners' wives. Mary Hannah Thomas had a strong, beautiful soprano she used to lead singing groups. She became the official greeter for the tent colony and roused spirits singing labor songs, such as this one with lyrics written by Frank Hayes, set to the tune of the Civil War song "The Battle Cry of Freedom":

We will win the fight today, boys,
We'll win the fight today,
Shouting the battle cry of union;
We will rally from the coal mines
We'll battle to the end,
Shouting the battle cry of union.
The union forever, hurrah! boys, hurrah!
Down with the Baldwins, up with the law;
For we're coming, Colorado, we're coming all the way,
Shouting the battle cry of union.

According to the UMW's records, 11,232 of Colorado's 13,980 coal miners went out on strike. About 9,000 of these worked the Trinidad field. These figures were confirmed in an independent count by the *Rocky Mountain News*.

Such a vast walkout shocked LaMont Bowers and Jesse Welborn, holed up in their Denver office. They apparently thought CFI miners were happy with the earlier concessions. Their subordinates had been telling them what they wanted to hear, just as Bowers and Welborn were telling the New York officers what they wanted to hear. True to form, the two seized on the explanation offered by their lawyers—that the union was intimidating workers into striking. They sent out bulletins stating that miners wishing to work—either old employees or newly hired ones—would be protected.

CFI also resorted to old tactics. The company's chief of security, William Reno, hired fifty more guards in Denver and sent them down to Trinidad. CFI furnished

John Lawson (second from right) *and Frank J. Hayes* (third from right) *stand with a group of UMW members in Colorado in 1913.* (Courtesy of the Denver Public Library, Western History Collection, X-60587.)

the guards with guns and paid them $3.50 a day. Reno also got Sheriff Farr to send deputies to the CFI camps in Huerfano County; Sheriff Jim Grisham did the same in Las Animas County.

The union was determined that strikebreakers would not be shipped in to take their jobs. The tent colonies had been placed where the miners could see non-strikers arriving. Frank Hayes had declared, "There will be no violence if our union can prevent it." But emotions ran high, particularly when it became clear that management had no intention of negotiating a settlement.

On September 25, five angry miners were damaging a company bridge when deputized mine guard Bob Lee came upon them. Lee was much despised by the miners, and when he drew his saddle rifle, one of the miners fired and instantly killed him.

The operators were outraged at Lee's killing. They blamed Mother Jones for "incendiary utterances" at a rally the evening before at Starkville. Several miners were rounded up by law enforcement, but none were ever charged with the murder.

CFI lawyers requested a grand jury to consider indicting the UMW on criminal charges. They said the UMW striking miners were violating the Sherman Antitrust Act (which was originally passed to keep railroads and other large corporations from forming trusts and erecting other barriers to competition) by preventing coal companies from fulfilling interstate contracts. In other words, the union was guilty of having a monopoly on the coal industry. The Justice Department responded by sending a special agent to investigate the charges.

The atmosphere grew more combustible each day. Miners' wives and children harassed strikebreaking workers. Buildings were dynamited, with each side accusing the other of setting the explosives. Miners and union organizers armed themselves by buying out the gun supplies at the local hardware stores and in Pueblo; high-powered Winchesters were the rifle of choice.

Both sides had spies reporting arms buying and movements. Most frightening to the union men were four machine guns brought in by the Baldwin-Felts men. The strikers began to watch what was coming in by automobile or by train. When huge searchlights arrived, the miners shot at the escort delivering them from the train station. A cowboy herding cattle nearby was killed in the cross fire.

John Lawson did what he could to minimize the violence. He appointed a leader for each of the twenty-one ethnic groups who could give clear explanations in their native languages to immigrants who did not speak English well.

When a bullet spattered dirt on the baseball field where miners were playing, the miners angrily ran for their guns. When shots were fired at the camp from a passing train, miners grabbed their rifles and chased the train. "Are you fellows crazy?" Lawson cried. "While you run down there a mile, the Hastings guards will come and take the tent colony." The miners grudgingly returned, their anger simmering in promises of revenge.

In another incident, Lawson found women and children standing at a fence cheering miners exchanging gunfire with guards behind a hill. He panicked at the thought of women and children being killed and ordered them back to the tents. He also organized the digging of holes beneath the wood floors of the tent homes for shelter from gunfire; still, days later two children were wounded in cross fire.

Lawson tried to be everywhere. He wore the miners' blue sweater and overalls with a soft cap pulled over the ears; since the guards scornfully called the immigrants "rednecks," Lawson made that a badge of pride. "Let every miner wear his red bandanna around his neck," he said. "It is our uniform." Like the rest, Lawson strapped a pistol at his waist.

Ethelbert Stewart, a federal mediator, came to Colorado to report events back to Washington and try to foster resolution if he could. He put it succinctly: "The only language common to all, and which all understand in southern Colorado, is the voice of the gun." Stewart had been appointed by the secretary of labor, who had been a UMW member. Stewart annoyed the operators to the point where they would not deal with him. For his part, Stewart said he could do nothing more because this was "a strike of the twentieth century against the tenth century mental attitude."

LaMont Bowers wrote Rockefeller Jr. that because miners had shot at guards and property, steps must be taken against them. He installed giant searchlights and soon 5,000 candlepower beams swept the tent colonies all night. Bowers also hired more guards. Eighteen gunfighters from New Mexico arrived by train. Sheriff Grisham deputized them before ordering the group to Ludlow.

When the gunfighters arrived, eight hundred union sympathizers and miners surrounded the men in the street and hustled them into union headquarters. After listening to the miners, the gunmen said they had been hired under false pretenses, turned in their badges to Sheriff Grisham, and returned to New Mexico on the next train.

Bowers pressured Governor Ammons for the Colorado militia "to drive the vicious agitators out of the state." The price of coal was increasing, and the citizens of Denver were unhappy about both higher prices and the violence. Ammons hated the strife, but he did not want to involve the Colorado National Guard. He was unsure the militia was necessary. Bowers got Denver bankers to promise Ammons they would lend the state money to pay for the militia.

On October 17, 1913, the operators introduced their newest weapon, an armored car for patrolling the mine country. Its sides were three-eighths of an inch thick, and it had two built-in machine guns. The miners called it the Death Special. The hated Belk and Belcher used it to open fire inside the Forbes tent colony. One miner was killed and a boy was shot nine times in the leg.

Men with rifles and artillery stand inside the armored car known as the Death Special as it patrols the tent colonies and mining camps during the strike. (Courtesy of the Denver Public Library, Western History Collection, X-60380.)

Ammons was deluged with telegrams protesting the Death Special. He decided to go to Trinidad. When he arrived on October 21, Mother Jones and her demonstrators sang the union song and carried signs reading, WE REPRESENT CFI SLAVES or THE DEMOCRATIC PARTY IS ON TRIAL. This referred to Ammons's election as a Democrat with strong support from working-class voters. If he intervened with the militia, or if the investigation called by the grand jury found the UMW in violation of the Sherman Antitrust Act, many Democratic voters might shift their support to the new Progressive Party.

Ammons toured the area for two days and decided not to involve the militia. He returned to Denver on October 23. The governor's situation had been complicated by his state auditor, Roady Kenehan, who had rejected the offer of a bank loan. Kenehan was a former blacksmith and staunch unionist who took office vowing to weed out corruption. He was large, loud, colorful, and fearless. He had also publicly proclaimed the Colorado militia to be led by dolts and liars.

Kenehan was primarily referring to General John Chase, head of the Colorado National Guard. Chase was a strong antiunionist who had done brutal and foolish things in earlier strikes when the militia was called in. In 1903 at Cripple Creek, he had arrested miners and jailed them without charges. In dramatic courtroom defiance, he had refused to obey the judge's order to release them. When court-martialed for willful disobedience, Chase had been found guilty and sentenced to dismissal from the Colorado National Guard. Then-governor James Peabody had signed his approval of the verdict but later set it aside when Chase's supporters vociferously protested. Peabody eventually restored Chase to his post.

In 1913, Chase was itching to break up another strike. He sent one of his officers to the strike zone to report back to him. This man was Lieutenant Karl Linderfelt, without doubt the most cruel militia officer in the state. In addition to being antiunion, Linderfelt also hated foreigners. Soon after his arrival, Linderfelt was deputized by Sheriff Grisham.

Serious skirmishing began on October 23, not long after Ammons left. In Walsenburg, a non-striking miner's

Lieutenant Karl Linderfelt (far right) *and his troop of the Colorado National Guard enter the Ludlow strike zone on horseback.* (Courtesy of the Denver Public Library, Western History Collection, Created by Stuart Mace, X-60538.)

wife found a threatening note pinned to her door: "If you don't move out of this neighborhood within 24 hours we will blow you out. Your husband is scabbing. We mean business." Terrified, she phoned the mine superintendent, who sent an escort to bring her and her belongings to camp property. They had to run a gauntlet of miners' wives and children shouting insults and throwing dirt. Sheriff's deputies surveying the scene fired shots without warning. When all had fled, three striking miners lay dead.

The violence escalated. When strikers tore up a section of track, mine guards fired on them. Mine guard

John Nimmo was killed and lay unnoticed in the snow-storm that swept in with the night. On October 27, a woman in Tabasco was killed by cross fire while making breakfast in her home, and her two children wounded. After that, strikers received guns and ammunition in cars supplied and driven by local union officials from Trinidad. A train hijacked by Baldwins was fired on by strikers dodging the searchlight beams. Several more strikers and guards were killed. Linderfelt sent tele-grams to Chase in Denver with phrases such as "looks hopeless" and "phone line in possession of rebels" and "no hope can be expected except only from troops."

Business leaders insisted Governor Ammons call out the militia. Desperately Ammons tried to make owners and union officers come to a compromise. He asked the operators of CFI, Rocky Mountain Fuel, and Victor-American to write out a settlement they could abide by and it would be presented to the union. At 8 PM on October 27, the companies pledged to continue to obey the state mining laws (listed specifically by title and number) and to give back jobs to all miners who could prove they had been innocent of any lawbreaking during the strike. There was no move to meet the union's de-mands. Obviously, the owners knew they had the gov-ernor on the run and the militia would soon be called out.

Ammons sent the proposal to Frank Hayes and his colleagues in Denver. They refused to accept it because union recognition was not in the settlement. Ammons now felt he had no choice. At 1:30 AM on October 28,

1913, he signed the order giving General Chase the authority to police the strike area with troops of the Colorado National Guard. Ammons justified his action by saying that it had "been made to appear to me by the peace officers of . . . counties of the state of Colorado . . . and by other good and reputable citizens . . . that there is a tumult threatened." He did order that the militia be limited to protecting mine property and the mine employees who chose to work. They were *not* to aid any new workers filling strikers' jobs.

It had taken just over a month for an impasse between the two sides to bring the strike into being and then to escalate into violence. The union leaders responded more to the "fight fire with fire" tactic than to their ideal of nonviolence. Now, with the Colorado militia under General Chase, a new ingredient had been added. Unfortunately, it would prove inflammatory.

7.
Martial Law

G eneral John Chase arrived at the coalfields on November 1, 1913, with 931 men. He had base camps at Trinidad and Walsenburg, with smaller units camped near various tent colonies of strikers. The first thing Chase ordered was for a military parade to be held near Ludlow.

Chase's orders from Governor Ammons were to protect non-striking miners who wished to work, to keep strikebreakers out, and to disarm all unauthorized persons. The last would not be easy. The miners were well armed by this time and did not want to give up their weapons. In Ludlow, only thirty-seven old rifles were surrendered. Lawson begged the strikers not to provoke the militiamen.

Captain Philip Van Cise was in charge of Ludlow. Van

General John Chase of the Colorado National Guard (left) *consults with Frank E. Gove, a member of CFI management.* (Courtesy of the Denver Public Library, Western History Collection, X-60525.)

Cise was a Denver lawyer who did not want a confrontation. He sent search parties into the colony for hidden guns, but he also talked with the strikers and scheduled baseball games and potluck meals with the miners and his men. But on November 8 near La Veta, the mixture of armed men and high tension brought about the incident Lawson so feared. It began when a non-striking miner was accosted by strikers with guns and bullied to join the union. He eluded them, found a telephone, and called for an escort home. The miners ambushed the escort car, killing three guards and the driver. The miner survived, crawling to a ranch for help.

Now General Chase had what he wanted—an incident of union violence he could use to justify taking action against the strikers. When, citing a lack of evidence, the district attorney of Las Animas County released four of the eight miners arrested for the shooting, Chase ordered their return to jail. He explained that he had supreme power under martial law. District Attorney John Hendricks was astounded. He hadn't heard that the governor had declared martial law. He telegraphed Governor Ammons in Denver. The timid governor asked General Chase for advice before declaring martial law. General Chase was now, in effect, a legal dictator.

Chase quickly set up a military tribunal. On November 15, he served District Attorney Hendricks notice that all persons arrested as military prisoners would be judged by seven men he had appointed. One of the judges was a mine operator's lawyer.

When President Woodrow Wilson was governor of New Jersey, he had been friendly to labor and pushed through some reform laws. On October 30, 1913, Wilson wrote the mine operators that he was "deeply disappointed" they had not come to an agreement with the miners. "The attention of the whole country," he wrote, was on "the distressing situation in the mines of the Colorado Fuel and Iron Company." Wilson's letter to CFI also complained about their treatment of federal mediator Ethelbert Stewart. He requested from the responsible

President Woodrow Wilson, a Democrat from New Jersey elected in 1913, played a complex role in the Ludlow strike, both encouraging the mine operators to come to an agreement with the strikers and supporting the use of the National Guard to stop the violence. (Library of Congress)

officers "a full and frank statement of the reasons that had led them to reject counsels of peace and accommodation in a matter now grown so critical."

LaMont Bowers replied with a six-page letter that accused Stewart of favoring the miners. He blamed the agitation on Mother Jones. Bowers acknowledged that what the strikers really wanted was union recognition. To this he declared, "We will never consent, if every mine is closed, the equipment destroyed, and the investment made worthless." Stewart replied simply, "Feudalism is no longer acceptable."

Meanwhile, Governor Ammons was ineffective. Auditor Roady Kenehan, determined to give every advantage to the union men, continued to find legalities to prevent releasing the militia's salaries. This sent General Chase to the mine operators and their sympathizers to borrow money to pay his men. Baldwin-Felts guards were enlisted in the militia, and the mine operators began insisting strikebreakers were necessary to mine coal for the approaching winter. On November 19, 1913, Ammons telegraphed President Wilson and Secretary of Labor William Wilson (no relation) for help. "I care not by what means," he said, for he felt the situation "growing worse hourly."

Wilson wrote another firm letter to Bowers: "I can only say that a word from you would bring the strike to an end, as all that is asked is that you agree to an arbitration by an unbiased board." The letter only infuriated Bowers. When labor secretary William Wilson pleaded with Rockefeller Jr. to intervene, Rockefeller replied that Bowers and Welborn were in charge.

On November 20, the Baldwin-Felts detective George Belcher was shot on a street in Trinidad. Belcher had been a marked man ever since he had gunned down Gerald Lippiatt in August. The shooter, Louis Zancanelli, who was paid $1,000 for the murder, knew Belcher wore a steel vest and would have to be shot in the head at close range. Zancanelli was arrested that night, and Chase's cavalry rode in the streets to prevent any further attacks or unrest. Under interrogation, Zancanelli confessed.

Labor secretary William Wilson persuaded the strike leaders to set aside their demand for union recognition for a while. He said he would try to secure the operators' approval of an arbitration committee appointed by the governor to deal with grievances.

Ammons got the operators to agree to a meeting by promising that union recognition would not be brought up. Wilson and Ammons talked with six representatives—three from each side—for fifteen hours on November 26-27. Their proposal was that the miners be granted all their demands except union recognition. The operators would have to agree to obey all state laws and to rehire the strikers, except for those whose jobs had been filled or who had been found guilty of lawbreaking. Expressing doubt that these three representatives accurately spoke for all the miners, the operators requested that the rank and file miners be allowed to vote. The referendum was prepared and explained to the striking miners in English, Spanish, Italian, Slavic, and Greek. Because it did not grant union recognition, the strikers voted it down on November 30. William Wilson went back to Washington, while the mine operators rejoiced that they had scored a public relations victory because the workers had rejected the settlement.

Governor Ammons, under intense pressure from the mine operators, changed his order to the militia. On November 30, he ordered military protection of new workers. "There is no excuse now for high prices," he said, "because the mines can be operated."

One of the worst Decembers in southeastern Colorado history blew in on December 3, 1913. Snow piled high in the colonies, causing many tent roofs to collapse from the weight. Families huddled around their stoves. Welborn wrote confidently to Rockefeller Jr. that the tent dwellers would soon be seeking work and conventional houses at the mine camps. He was wrong.

The militia troopers suffered, too. They had to endure similar tent conditions, and while the miners were paid weekly from UMW funds, auditor Roady Kenehan was doing everything he could to hold back the soldiers' pay. He thundered that he examined *all* expenditures, and he would not authorize taxpayers' money for "officers' shindigs," which included $11 for a cocktail.

The withheld funds posed no difficulty for officers such as Chase and Linderfelt, but the troopers had to endure unusual hardship. Their boots were worn through and their uniforms had become ragged. Without wages,

The snowbound tent colony at Ludlow during the stormy December of 1913. (Courtesy of the Denver Public Library, Western History Collection, X-60339.)

their families were denied income, for the militia had to leave their regular jobs when called up by the Colorado National Guard. On Thanksgiving, they had angrily burned Roady Kenehan in effigy while their band played "There'll Be a Hot Time in the Old Town Tonight." Kenehan was in the area on an inspection tour. He asked to be taken to the spot where his effigy was buried. He stood on it and shouted to the militiamen, "Sure, and I'm the only man in this world who ever stood on his own grave!" He laughed. "You boys have had fun," he said, "but remember, you can only buy your horses once if you don't want me to burn your backsides."

In early December, the first strikebreakers arrived. They came from as near as Missouri and as far east as Pittsburgh. Some could not read, some had no idea they were breaking a strike, and all desperately wanted to work. They were guaranteed $3.08 a day and railroad passage. By the end of the month, 9,600 had been brought in, equal to the number of strikers; most lodged in company buildings the strikers had vacated. Soon Welborn reported operations were fairly normal.

On the other side, Lawson and Hayes were worried about the spirits of the men and the future of the strike. At this point, Ed Doyle's records showed 19,300 men, women, and children on strike relief. The national UMW officers in Indianapolis were upset by the lack of progress and reports of union connection to the assassination of Belcher. General Chase had jailed forty-three miners on charges ranging from murder and buying guns to

Boys in Ludlow stand next to the effigy of Roady Kenehan built by frustrated National Guard troops. (Courtesy of the Denver Public Library, Western History Collection, X-60344.)

inciting the overthrow of society. Their citizenship rights, such as seeing lawyers, making appeals, or receiving visitors, had been suspended under martial law.

The State Federation of Labor was concerned too, and called a special convention in Denver on December 16, 1913, to discuss the possibility of recalling Governor Ammons and removing General Chase. At the convention, Mother Jones was on hand to stop calls for moderation. She declared her hatred for the rich and advocated the hanging of Governor Ammons. She invited everyone to march with her to the capitol to confront him.

Two thousand marchers joined her the next day, marching behind a banner marked LUDLOW and singing hymns. An agitated Ammons defensively told them that they should present him with legal proof that Chase was in league with the coal operators and was unjustly treating the strikers. The delegates took him up on this, and Ammons gave John Lawson permission for a six-man commission and a letter of authority to receive cooperation from the National Guard.

Christmas came and went. In Denver, spirits were high. In the tent colonies, families were discouraged. While General Chase showed his officers at the Trinidad mess hall a silver saddle he had received from some of them, the miners' children received only fruit and candy distributed by John Lawson.

On December 30, near Ludlow, a group of militia went on horseback to pull a car out of a snow bank. One horse tripped on barbed wire hidden by the snow and badly injured its rider. Lieutenant Karl Linderfelt took over, determined to punish strikers for what he said was a cruel trap set by the miners. Linderfelt had been part of the U.S. force that put down Filipinos during the Philippine insurrection of 1899-1900, and he had been a mercenary in 1910 during a revolution in Mexico. Now he rounded up suspects. One was Louis Tikas, an educated Greek from the University of Athens, who was the translator for the Greek miners and the most trusted advisor to all the immigrants.

Lawson was alarmed when he heard that Linderfelt had arrested Tikas. He sent a telegram to Ammons saying,

> We have reason to believe that it is [Linderfelt's] deliberate purpose to provoke the strikers to bloodshed he has threatened to kill Louis Tikas. . . .

On January 4, when Mother Jones arrived in Trinidad, Chase had soldiers arrest her at the station and put her on the next train back to Denver. He announced he would arrest her and suspend her civil rights if she returned. On January 11, 1914, Mother Jones returned. Chase personally arrested her and, with cavalry escort, deposited her at San Rafael Hospital, where she was closely guarded under "military surveillance."

Ten days later, a protest march to the hospital was organized. Chase said he heard that the miners' wives

Women march in protest against the arrest of Mother Jones and in support of the UMW strike in January 1914. The sashes they wear read "Trinidad."
(Courtesy of the Denver Public Library, Western History Collection, X-60505.)

were going to liberate Mother Jones. Leading a cavalry unit himself, he shouted for the marchers to halt. His horse was skittish and reared. The general fell off. The troopers rode right into the marchers to disperse them. They swung their weapons, leaving some women slashed by sabers or bruised from rifle stocks.

One Denver paper's headline read GREAT CZAR FELL! AND IN FURY TOLD TROOPS TO TRAMPLE WOMEN.

John Lawson sent a telegram to Frank Hayes at the UMW convention in Indianapolis. It was filled with wild exaggerations that Lawson had accepted in good faith from witnesses:

> . . . General Chase . . . issued orders to shoot the women and children and shoot to kill . . . militiamen jab sabers and bayonets into back of women with babes in arms and trample them under the feet of their horses. . . .

When Hayes leaped to the platform and read it, he sparked rage and determination to continue helping the Colorado strikers. In Washington, DC, Colorado congressman Ed Keating, who had been elected on the promise to restore fair government in the southeastern district, was finally able to get a congressional investigation of the strike.

Congressman Martin D. Foster, a doctor from Illinois, was appointed chairman of the investigation sponsored by the House Subcommittee on Mines and Mining. Hence, this investigation is referred to as the Foster Committee. Foster wasted no time starting. The first hearings were on February 9, 1914, in Denver. The

Colorado state geologist gave a background on coal resources and mines. The chief mine inspector explained how his office was understaffed and unable to monitor safety violations adequately. The Colorado labor commissioner testified that coal operators controlled many political and civil offices. Albert Felts of the Baldwin-Felts Agency testified that he hired guards without checking into their pasts and that he knew only one sheriff who would not deputize his agents. He admitted having four machine guns and the Death Special armored car at Trinidad.

As the hearings went on, Auditor Roady Kenehan continued to object to bills submitted by the National Guard, blaming General Chase for inadequate receipts. At the end of February, the governor withdrew all but two hundred troops from the strike zone to keep expenses down.

The months of March and April saw three major events. On March 10, 1914, a strikebreaker was found dead by the railroad tracks. The train crew said he had wandered drunk in front of the locomotive, but Chase claimed strikers had beaten him and laid him on the tracks. Chase ordered his men to go to the nearby tent colony of Forbes and tear down the tents. He said bloodhounds had followed a scent there.

Mother Jones was the focus of the second event. She was finally released from her ten weeks under guard in San Rafael Hospital in Trinidad and sent to Denver on a train. General Chase forbade her to return. Of course, she did, and Chase intercepted her and had her locked in the Walsenburg courthouse basement.

The third event occurred when General Chase accepted a local company of mine guards, mine bosses, and vigilantes into the militia. These men were sworn in by Linderfelt and received neither military training nor uniforms. These irregulars were designated Troop A.

Meanwhile, the Foster Committee had finished its interviews in Colorado and returned to Washington, DC. It called up John D. Rockefeller Jr., who testified on April 6, 1914. He declared that he trusted LaMont Bowers and saw no point in interfering with his management. He refused to bargain with any union.

8.
War

In the Ludlow tent colony, the Greek miners celebrated their Orthodox Church Easter on April 19. The day was warm enough for baseball, and Ludlow men and their wives played and then enjoyed music and dancing.

Monday morning, April 20, 1914, Major Patrick Hamrock was given a note from a strikebreaker's wife saying that her husband was being held hostage by strikers in Ludlow. Hamrock sent three men to investigate. They returned having found nothing and with word from Louis Tikas that no such man was in the colony.

Hamrock then ordered Tikas to come talk to him. Hamrock thought that Tikas was "a restraining influence." Captain Philip Van Cise said Tikas was "the greatest single agent for peace during the strike." It was generally believed that of all the immigrant groups in the camps, the Greeks, many of whom had fought in war in their native land, were the quickest to retaliate to attacks or to strike out at perceived threats. The earlier arrest of Tikas had made him a lightning rod. The Greek strikers wanted to protect him and were convinced there was a plan to have him arrested or killed. Despite this perceived threat, Tikas agreed to meet Hamrock at the train depot, a neutral place. Hamrock then ordered the company's machine gun to be brought to him.

At 8:50 AM, Tikas told Hamrock and the wife, now in the depot too, that the woman's husband no longer lived in the colony. But as he spoke, strikers with guns began to converge on the depot and take positions in arroyos or along ridges outside the town of Ludlow.

As a new group of militia approached, Tikas realized the danger and, in an attempt to maintain peace, hurried back to the tent colony, waving his handkerchief and yelling for the men to disperse. He had promised the meeting would be calm. Hamrock went to call General Chase.

As he was on the telephone, Hamrock heard gunfire. It is not known who fired the first shot, but a battle had begun. The women gathered their children and took shelter in the pits John Lawson had earlier ordered dug underneath floors. Others fled to the pump station and, when bullets peppered the facility, descended to platforms in the well. By 9:30 the shooting was everywhere. Louis Tikas got to the office tent and telephoned John

Members of the Colorado National Guard lie in wait with their guns, which include an automatic rifle on a tripod, on Water Tank Hill near Ludlow. The tracks of the Colorado & Southern Railway can be seen just in front of them. (Courtesy of the Denver Public Library, Western History Collection, created by Stuart Mace, X-60554.)

Lawson in Trinidad for help. On his side, Major Hamrock phoned General Chase in Denver and was told to hold his position until reinforcements arrived.

The battle raged into the afternoon. The strikers had more men, but the militia had superior guns. Extra help for the militia came from the south in the form of union haters deputized by Sheriff Grisham. The drivers of the cars they hijacked testified later that these men talked of clearing out the strikers and burning the tent homes.

About 5:00 PM, the militiamen were strafing the tents with machine gun fire. At one point, sensing a lull, the Snyder family came out of their pit to get food and water. A bullet hit eleven-year-old Frank in the head. They had no choice but to jump back into the pit with their dead son.

Sometime between 5:30 and 6:00 PM, the tents began burning. The flames might have been started by the gunfire, but an officer later testified that "men and soldiers swarmed into the tent colony and deliberately assisted the conflagration by spreading the fire from tent to tent. . . . Beyond a doubt, it was seen to, intentionally, that the fire should destroy the whole of the colony." The colony women reported seeing men using flaming brooms dipped in coal oil to set fire to the tent homes. The soldiers stated later that they thought the burning homes were abandoned.

Whether any specific individual ordered the burning of the tents remains a mystery. National Guard officers

Smoke clouds the sky as the miners camp at the Forbes Mine burns during the Ludlow battle. (Library of Congress)

said one tent caught fire and the wind spread it. But there was little wind, and the officer's testimony quoted above described men methodically setting individual fires. Another officer admitted that the men had "ceased to be an army and become a mob."

Women and children fled from the shallow pits and the inferno above them. Thanks to a local freight train that stopped between the militia and the colony, the refugees were able to make it safely to an arroyo. The Snyder family carried the body of their dead son wrapped in a white sheet. Linderfelt allowed them to take refuge in the train station. The other women and children driven from the pits shivered through the cold April night with nothing but the clothes on their backs.

Back in Ludlow, the miners and the militia continued to exchange fire. Around 9:00 PM, some militiamen screamed, "We've got Louie the Greek!" and brought him with two others to Linderfelt. When Linderfelt cursed the prisoners, Tikas cursed him back, and Linderfelt smashed Tikas with his rifle so heavily that the stock split. Tikas staggered back; despite his slight build, he did not fall, though the blow had left his skull bared. There were cries to hang Tikas, and someone threw a rope over a telegraph pole. Linderfelt called for orderly behavior; he then left for the railroad depot to collect men for another assault. He ordered Sergeant Cullen to guard Tikas's life, but Cullen abandoned the prisoners to two militiamen as soon as Linderfelt was out of sight.

The prisoners and their guards stood illuminated by

the burning tents. The guards later claimed that the miners began firing at them and they fled, leaving the prisoners behind. This story was never confirmed, but it is certain that all three prisoners were shot dead. Inquest evidence showed that Tikas had been shot three times in the back with steel-jacket bullets from the soldiers' Springfields, but that the fatal bullet was a soft-nosed that could have come from an irregular in Troop A or from a miner's gun. No one could say whether Tikas was caught in the crossfire or whether he was executed. The militiamen who stood to be blamed were the only ones to provide testimony.

Gunfire continued sporadically through the night. Most of the guards joined Major Hamrock in the train station to await General Chase's reinforcements from Denver. In the hills east of Ludlow, the miners met up with Lawson's volunteers from Trinidad, who had packed themselves into five gondola cars on a freight train.

The dawn of April 21 revealed the saddest toll of the night's violence. Four women and their eleven children had gathered into one pit, the largest, but it was not large enough. A burning bed collapsed on the opening, followed by roofing debris, and they could not escape their 350 cubic feet of air space. Two of the women and all of the children were asphyxiated by the oily smoke. The Ludlow postmistress, Susan Hollearan, found Mary Petrucci, one of the fire pit survivors, wandering in the ruins of the smoking colony. The debris above the pit had burned to ashes, and she had gotten out. She was

Not long after the battle, a man inspects the underground shelter at Ludlow where two women and eleven children died during the fire. All across the colony, miners' families had sought shelter in pits and cellars such as this one. (Courtesy of the Denver Public Library, Western History Collection, X-60482.)

confused and unable to say where her children were or what had happened. Soon, the other survivor, Alcarita Pedregon, appeared, and Hollearan put them both on a train to Trinidad.

Hollearan then woke Linderfelt at the depot with his men and led them in a search of pits. It was afternoon before they found the two dead women and the eleven children, ranging in age from three months to nine years. The corpses were not removed until Wednesday. When the undertaker's wagons came from Trinidad, they were fired upon. The bodies of Louis Tikas and his fellow miners had been left by the railroad tracks.

The fatalities of the battle now numbered twenty-four: the thirteen in the pit, Louis Tikas and four other miners, little Frank Snyder, one militiaman, three mine guards, and one passerby.

Once the news of the horrors at Ludlow spread, the strikers became enraged. Even Lawson gave in to the fury. Referring to the "horrible atrocities," he proclaimed, "We now have the sinews of war backed by guns and ammunition and the faith and financial backing of every labor-union man in the country. . . . The murder of men and women at Ludlow . . . has cinched the determination to fight to a finish."

Miners swarmed from the canyons and hills. They did not have telephone or telegraph communication. Some groups acted on their own, others under Lawson's direction. They attacked the mines, blowing up buildings and mine entrances. Their strategy was to destroy property rather than confront the militia.

Ed Doyle was in Denver when the first news came through. He immediately sent telegrams to Colorado politicians and labor leaders: "For God's sake and in the name of humanity. . . . Miners, their wives and children, are being slaughtered by the dozen." The Colorado State Federation of Labor sent out a "Call to Arms" asking local unions to form volunteer companies "to protect the workers of Colorado against murder and cremation of men, women, and children by armed assassins in the employ of coal companies . . . serving under the guise of militiamen." The plan was for preparation only at this point. "We expect to break no law; we intend to exercise our lawful right as citizens, to defend our homes and our constitutional rights." The call was printed in all Colorado papers. It also requested that spare arms be sent to the State Federation of Labor headquarters in Denver.

LaMont Bowers reported to John D. Rockefeller Jr. that the gunfight resulted from an attack on the militia by the miners and said that the fires were started by explosions of dynamite hidden in the tents. Governor Ammons was in Washington, DC, when his lieutenant-governor telegraphed him begging for instructions. General Chase and the mine operators were screaming for more militia, but there must be a guarantee, too, that the militia would be paid. Ammons wired back that he would get the money somehow and that Chase should be given authority to do what he wanted. Ammons caught the next train home.

Chase had problems mustering new militiamen. He called up six hundred on April 22, but only 362 showed up at the armory in Denver. Seventy-six guardsmen of Troop C refused to depart until paid their back wages. Chase threatened them with court-martial, but they did not budge. The troop train left without them on April 23, with sharpshooters in the locomotive and additional ammunition and field guns. Six train crews had to be called before one was found willing to run the train.

As the train rolled south, it was paralleled by a caravan of four cars carrying guns and ammunition for the strikers, sent by the Colorado Federation of Labor. Despite an accident on the rain-slick road, the union men got to Walsenburg before the troop train.

Finally back in Denver, Governor Ammons was con-
fronted by one thousand members of the Women's Peace
Association, led by Colorado state senator Helen Ring
Robinson. The entire day of April 25, they camped and
sang at the Capitol. They demanded that Ammons ask
President Wilson for federal troops to replace the militia
they believed was out of control. At 6:30 PM, Ammons
reported to the president that he could not increase the
Colorado militia beyond 650 men, and that to quell the
insurrection he needed a battalion of infantry and a
troop of cavalry. He gave the constitutional requirement
for intervention as "an industrial controversy between
interstate organizations with headquarters outside
Colorado."

9.
Defeat

April 25 in Trinidad was burial day for the Ludlow fire victims. Bells tolled as the procession of two black caskets and eleven white ones moved to the cemetery. The UMW had sent money for the funerals. On April 27, Louis Tikas was honored. Four Greeks swore ritual vengeance and pounded the floor of the undertaker's chapel with their rifle stocks. The silent procession to the cemetery was a mile long. That evening the militia sent men to Walsenburg, where several hundred strikers were wrecking a mine.

On April 28, two days after the request from Governor Ammons, President Wilson ordered federal troops sent to Colorado. He let Ammons know that it was a temporary measure and that Colorado would have to handle its own problems very soon. He did not want to be

Hundreds of coal miners marched in the funeral procession for Louis Tikas. Here the procession moves down North Commercial Street in Trinidad. (Courtesy of the Denver Public Library, Western History Collection, created by Lewis R. Dold, X-60441.)

misinterpreted by increasingly strong labor voters as a strikebreaker.

In the intervening two days, Wilson had tried once again to negotiate with the Rockefellers. There were now huge protests sweeping the U.S. against them, including outside the New York City offices and John D. Rockefeller Jr.'s private residence. Wilson hoped this might soften CFI for a settlement, but he was wrong.

The strikers had been crying "Remember Ludlow!" as they attacked mines and then disappeared into the hills. At Forbes Mine, for example, they gutted the camp and killed nine defenders; the miners also lost men.

Federal troops from Fort Robinson, Nebraska, arrived in Trinidad on April 30. Wilson's proclamation, printed in newspapers and on posters, ordered all men bearing arms to disperse and return home peaceably. Within a week, 1,590 federal troops and 61 officers were in the area. They had general directives from the secretary of war: 1) no group should expect special privileges, 2) everyone but U.S. troops must surrender weapons, and 3) all gun shops and saloons in the strike area must close. The Colorado militia companies went home. Then came the torrential spring rains. The rivers and arroyos roiled with rain and the spring snowmelt washing down from the Rockies.

The bloody events in Colorado were named the Ludlow Massacre by a UMW publiscist in Denver. Public opinion swelled against CFI and the Rockefellers, the most hated of the capitalist families. There was continued picketing at 26 Broadway in New York City, with crowds wearing black armbands to commemorate the dead at Ludlow. They followed John D. Rockefeller Jr. wherever he went, even to church. The public was further stirred by a traveling group of Ludlow women and children. The reformer and novelist Upton Sinclair sparked the idea of Ludlow survivors visiting President Wilson and telling him firsthand what they experienced. The women were willing, and Sinclair raised travel money at a mass rally on the capitol grounds in Denver. They left in the company of a distinguished Colorado judge, Ben Lindsey. Sinclair handled publicity.

The massacre at Ludlow made the June 1914 cover of the monthly publication *The Masses, a Socialist journal founded in 1911 and edited by leftist writer Max Eastman. The dramatic cover image of an armed miner holding a dead child was drawn by renowned American artist John Sloan.* (Library of Congress)

The climax of their tour was an appearance at a mass meeting at Beethoven Hall in New York City. There were speeches, though Mary Petrucci, who had survived the pit, never spoke. She was still in mental and emotional shock.

Though Ludlow miners and their families were receiving great emotional support, things were not well with the union itself. The national officers of the UMW in Indianapolis had sent Ed Doyle $15,000 to pay for funerals and to rebuild the tent colony. Then Doyle asked for more money to buy guns, and Frank Hayes suggested a national strike to support southeastern Colorado. These requests seemed extreme to the national officers, who had to be concerned with the entire union. The UMW had a new strike looming in Ohio, and the rival, radical International Workers of the World was pushing for influence there and elsewhere. The national UMW board felt it was time to end the Colorado strike and accept defeat. They were just about bankrupt. In late April 1914, the national UMW issued a surprising public statement saying that recognition of the unions was not the barrier to settlement; it was not even an issue. A further discouragement was that, despite public outrage against Rockefeller, the CFI mines were running with new workers. Production was 80 percent of former output.

The National Guard's investigation of the Ludlow battle revealed that Major Hamrock had deliberately turned a machine gun on the colony and the militia had methodically set fire to the tent homes, and that Lieutenant Linderfelt had wrongly antagonized the miners with his treatment of Louis Tikas and in other ways. Yet, when these officers and twenty others were court-martialed before General Chase's tribunal, they were all acquitted except for Linderfelt, who received a slight demotion for his treatment of Louis Tikas. John Lawson was the only witness called from the miners' side. With the innocent verdict in the court-martial, the National Guard was officially exonerated. None were ever tried in a civilian court.

Using his power as top prosecuting official in the state, Colorado attorney general Fred Farrar set out to try the union leaders of District 15 for the violence and lawlessness in the strike, including the twenty-four deaths during the Ludlow battle. First, Judge Jesse Northcutt called a grand jury in Las Animas County to investigate evidence in order to get indictments. Witnesses were called in, and on August 29, a grand jury composed of CFI employees, deputy sheriffs, and six local merchants reported that "crimes were committed by armed mobs . . . of the UMW and its sympathizers" who had "bought the guns and ammunition and directed criminal activities." John Lawson's name led the list of 124 indicted.

Meanwhile, federal troops kept the peace. Saloons stayed closed, men were disarmed, and no new miners were allowed in from outside Colorado. Only Colorado citizens and miners working before the Ludlow battle could work. Operators, owners, unionists, politicians, clergymen, and citizens all petitioned Wilson to keep the troops there.

In early September 1914, President Wilson made another effort to end the strike. He submitted the Fairley-Davies truce plan, named for its appointed writers, to the operators of the three largest Colorado mines and to the officers of the UMW. The plan called for a three-year truce, during which the mining laws would be enforced, law-abiding striking miners would be rehired, and mines would have their own grievance committees. A three-man panel appointed by the president would arbitrate local conflicts.

Despite their general lack of unanimity, the UMW representatives accepted the Fairley-Davies truce on September 15, and the strikers ratified it. The operators, confident that they had won the strike, rejected it. They said it was "unfair to our workmen" to replace them with striking miners, and they did not accept the idea of arbitration. Welborn explained, "No commission, no matter how impartial, would be as competent as the natural managing officers of a company to say how its properties should be operated."

President Wilson and the miners were furious. The miners had even given up their prime goal of union recognition. On October 5, when the operators had made it clear they were not interested in a settlement, the UMW suggested that President Wilson take over the mines. Wilson declined, unsure that he had the constitutional right to do so.

On November 19, with winter coming on, Frank Hayes told President Wilson that the UMW was out of money.

He asked Wilson to end the strike in a manner allowing the UMW to save face and to feel they had been honorable. The president agreed. He set up a settlement commission which would persevere—even if the operators would not accept its mediations. "At least," the president said, he could "create the instrumentality by which like troubles and disputes may be amicably and honorably settled in the future."

Along with Wilson's proclamation, the UMW officers sent their comments to the miners:

> We deem it the part of wisdom . . . to terminate the strike. . . . All lovers of liberty and believers in fair play . . . must admire the heroic struggle of the Colorado miners against the great wealth and influence of Rockefeller and his associates. We believe that our people have not died in vain. . . . We recognize no surrender.

On December 7, 1914, the Colorado delegates voted unanimously to end the strike. The miners did not protest. Fourteen months had been enough. Some of the miners went back to work. Others drifted out of state. There were no more strike benefits. Gradually the tent homes came down. Within a month the federal troops were gone.

Although the strike was officially over, the courts of Colorado, still under the influence of mine operators, were determined to prosecute the union and its leaders. On February 15, 1915, in the Trinidad District Court,

Colorado attorney general Fred Farrar charged John Lawson and ten others with the murder of mine guard John Nimmo. The killing, on October 25 or 26, 1913, had occurred early in the strike when the Death Special had roamed, shooting into the tent colonies. Nimmo had been found lying in the snow, and a former deputy sheriff provided the written, signed testimony necessary for a murder charge.

The judge of the Trinidad District Court had just been appointed by new governor George Carlson, who was elected in November 1914 when the exhausted Elias Ammons decided not to run again. The new judge was Granby Hillyer, who had been an attorney for coal companies. The prosecuting attorney was Frank West, who had ridden on duty in the Death Special.

Republican governor George Carlson won his seat in 1914 as the result of a split among Progressive and Democratic party voters in Colorado, over issues such as the Ludlow Massacre and Prohibition. (Library of Congress)

On March 26, 1915, Louis Zancanelli's trial for the murder of the Baldwin-Felts agent George Belcher ended with a hung jury. For the new trial, Judge Hillyer ordered the jury be selected from a list provided by the Las Animas County sheriff, instead of from the general population. This list was of people known to detest the strikers. Not surprisingly, this new jury found Zancanelli guilty, and he was sentenced to life imprisonment with hard labor.

On April 21, 1915, John Lawson's trial began. Lawson was not accused of firing the shot that killed Nimmo, but of being the union leader at Ludlow on the day Nimmo was killed. Frank West presented his witnesses, including Lieutenant Karl Linderfelt and hired guards who had been in the action that day. In cross-examination, defense lawyer Horace Hawkins showed that several of the guards had never seen John Nimmo until he was dead. Hawkins also questioned the credibility of witnesses hired as mercenaries from other states. Despite this spirited defense, John Lawson was found guilty.

Hawkins immediately asked for thirty days to file for a new trial. Judge Hillyer turned him down and sentenced Lawson to life imprisonment even as the Colorado Supreme Court was considering a petition to prevent Judge Hillyer from hearing any more strike cases because of his antiunion prejudice.

Lawson's conviction set off protests across the U.S. If Lawson could be condemned for the killing of a man he had never seen, why wasn't Rockefeller, whose money paid for gunmen who participated in the Ludlow burning and other strike killings, charged with murder? Former U.S. Senator Thomas Patterson, along with a Denver businessman, put up the $35,000 bond for Lawson to go free upon the appeal of his trial.

The national attention paid to John Lawson's trial led to further divisions within the UMW. There was jealousy and internal dissension and even an ugly split between former strike leaders Frank Hayes and Ed Doyle.

While Lawson was awaiting his appeal hearing, the political winds in Colorado shifted. Early in the summer of 1916, the Colorado Supreme Court declared that votes in the November 1914 elections from the coal camp precincts of Huerfano County were invalid because of mine company interference in the voting. The precincts had been on private mine property, and all voter registration records were kept in company offices. Sheriff Jeff Farr was removed from office, and the valid winner, E. L. Neelly, replaced him.

Before the November 1916 elections, Governor George Carlson and Attorney General Farrar, realizing that labor had gained political strength, quashed the indictments of the miners who had yet to be tried. But it was too late to save their careers; both Carlson and Farrar lost the election.

The new governor and attorney general filed a brief to the Colorado Supreme Court pointing out numerous errors in the case and trial of John Lawson. On April 20, 1917, the Supreme Court, citing the extreme prejudicial circumstances in the first trial, reversed the conviction. Lawson was a free man.

Having been cold-shouldered out of the UMW, John Lawson took a job recruiting miners for the Victor-American Company. Then he took a job as vice president with Rocky Mountain Fuel Company, whose new owner was progressive industrial and social reformer Josephine Roche. At his new job in management, Lawson put his belief in collective bargaining into practice when he drew up contracts for Rocky Mountain Fuel's miners with the UMW. He also directed an insurance firm for coal companies.

Over four hundred miners who had initially been charged never came to trial. Four convictions were over-turned, all due to irregularities during trial. Zancanelli's conviction was overturned when it became known one juror had made a bet on a guilty verdict. Zancanelli was never retried. Baldwin-Felts detective Walter Belk was tried for a pre-strike crime and was acquitted.

In April 1917, the month John Lawson became a free man, in one of the last events directly connected with the strike, the United States declared war on Germany. President Wilson declared that joining the war effort with the European Allies would be America's contribu-tion to making the world "safe for democracy."

10.

Consequences

After the battle at Ludlow, John D. Rockefeller Jr. slowly began to realize he had been given bad advice and information. He had wanted to prove himself to his father and to maintain the Rockefeller way of managing their businesses. However, after the deaths at Ludlow, he learned that Bowers and Welborn had never gone to the coalfields but had accepted what their regional manager in Pueblo told them. Then he learned to his horror that the manager they listened to had not gone to the coalfields either; he had simply passed along what mine superintendents, security guards, and company-sympathetic politicians and sheriffs had told him. Rockefeller continued to defend his position, but the public protests and outcries eventually got to him. The final straw might have been a time-bomb-in-the-making that blew up in a New York building. It was said the bomb was intended for Rockefeller's city house and was being prepared by four members of the radical International Workers of the World (who were killed in the explosion). Rockefeller Jr. hired detectives to guard his family but began to wonder about the depth of the hatred. Was it simply due to jealousy, as his father had always insisted? Or were he and his family somehow responsible?

Rockefeller had always thought of his family as generous philanthropists committed to helping people through the Rockefeller Foundation. He began to consider modifying his father's staunch no-response-to-criticism policy. He decided to hire a publicist to create a more favorable image for the Rockefeller family and, through the Rockefeller Foundation, to fund a scientific study of labor-management relations to create a formula for industrial harmony in the future.

Most critically, Rockefeller hired William Lyon Mackenzie King, a Canadian who had been recommended to Rockefeller by Harvard president Charles Eliot. As a graduate student, King had studied sociology at the University of Chicago and economics at Harvard. He had tried to activate practical reforms, such as alerting Canada's government that militia uniforms were made under sweatshop conditions. A policy was then enacted requiring all suppliers to pay fair wages and maintain safe working conditions. A deeply devout Presbyterian, King became convinced that God had

Following his work with Rockefeller, William Lyon Mackenzie King returned to Canada in 1917 to pursue a political career. He would eventually serve a lengthy tenure as prime minister. (Library of Congress)

chosen him to be a reformer. King believed that society and government should have the power to limit—but not control—extreme imbalances of power and wealth in society.

When King graduated from Harvard in 1900, he was offered a faculty position. He chose instead to return to Canada to organize and edit a government paper, the *Labour Gazette*. In 1907, he drafted what became Canada's basic labor law, the Industrial Disputes Investigation Act, which establishes the state as "an impartial umpire" in industrial relations. At age thirty-five, in 1909, King was named head of the newly formed Ministry of Labor, where he drafted legislation and attempted to deal with Canada's labor disputes. When Prime Minister Wilfrid Laurier was voted out in 1911, King, a Laurier appointee, lost his job, too.

In 1914, King was the same age as John D. Rockefeller Jr. At their first meeting that June, Rockefeller felt an instant rapport. "My first impression of him was overwhelming," he recalled years later. Their personalities complemented each other; where Rockefeller was formal and a little defensive, King was warm, charming, and clever.

Though he needed a job, King was uneasy about the Rockefeller connection. He did not want to compromise his principles. But after their second meeting, King judged Rockefeller Jr. as "uncomplicated and well intentioned" and deeply rooted in moral and religious feelings. On August 1, 1914, King agreed to work for the Rockefeller Foundation and to advise Rockefeller.

In his diary, King said he wanted to convince

Rockefeller that there was "a new spirit abroad." Labor and capital could work together. King also taught Rockefeller a new style of management. Problems should be dealt with proactively, before they festered into conflict. He worked with Rockefeller to find new ways to compromise and reach agreements.

Another new element in labor-capital relations had actually been created by President William Howard Taft in 1911 and approved by Congress in 1912. The Industrial Relations Commission (IRC) had, as American political essayist Walter Lippmann put it, "the task of explaining why America, supposed to have become the land of promise, has become the land of disappointment and deep-seated discontent." Its nine-member panel, appointed by the president, had authority to explore the origins of industrial disorder, report them to Congress, and prescribe remedies which Congress could choose to enact into law.

In 1913, President Wilson appointed the first members, including the first woman to serve on a federal commission—Daisy Harriman, a wealthy supporter of Wilson and social reforms. Wilson made Frank P. Walsh of Missouri the IRC chairman. Walsh had been recommended for his legal ability, vigor, and support of labor.

By 1914, the IRC had investigators in Colorado. They sought testimony from the Ludlow wives and Judge Lindsey in New York City. Lindsey was ready to begin public testimony sessions in Denver in December 1914, as the strike was close to an end, when John Lawson and

Ed Doyle brought him an April 30 telegram. The telegram seemed to show that John D. Rockefeller Jr., contrary to what he had testified before the Foster Committee, had actually been giving Bowers and Welborn advice during the strike. When Jesse Welborn was called to testify, Walsh waved the telegram in front of him and asked if he had received it. Welborn said he had. Walsh then subpoenaed all correspondence during the strike between CFI in Denver and Rockefeller headquarters in New York City.

By January 1915, Walsh was in New York City facing down John D. Rockefeller Jr. Whereas Martin Foster had questioned witnesses with a medical doctor's gentleness, Frank Walsh, according to one historian, was like an inquisitor with a blowtorch.

But John D. Rockefeller Jr., under the influence of Mackenzie King, had a surprise. He had already pushed LaMont Bowers into retirement. Entering the committee room, he was calm and confident. He began by reading an opening statement prepared by King. He said he believed in the right of workers to belong to unions, just as managers could belong to their own organizations. However, he continued, that was not the same as the right of the union to bargain with management.

Under questioning about specifics in Colorado, Rockefeller testified once again to the company policy of giving managers the independence to run CFI and trusting the truth of their reports. But he pointed to his hiring of a publicist as evidence of a new attitude that corporations must make more details public. No matter what he was asked, Rockefeller remained courteous and patient. The next day he shook hands with Mother Jones and invited her to his office. She admitted to being bowled over by his testimony. Rockefeller jokingly told her to stop throwing compliments. She replied, "I am more inclined to throw bricks."

Walsh was not satisfied by this new Rockefeller and assailed him about his comment that corporations should not deduct union dues from wages. "I should think," Rockefeller said, "that any company would somewhat hesitate to deduct from the wages of its men in the interest of some other institution."

Walsh leaped. "Are you aware that the Colorado Supply Company has such deductions made from the wages of men covering bills at their store?"

Rockefeller Jr. said no. He added that his views on an owner's moral responsibility were changing. "I should hope that I could never reach the point where I would not be constantly progressing to something higher, better—both with reference to my own acts and . . . to the general situation in the company. My hope is that I am progressing. It is my desire to." This closing comment drew applause. The next day he spent over an hour with Mother Jones and also met with union officials, including Lawson, Doyle, and Hayes.

Lawson was not impressed with this new Rockefeller. In his testimony he told the IRC that Rockefeller's philanthropies were not generosity: "It is not their money

Frank P. Walsh, chairman of the Industrial Relations Commission. (Library of Congress)

that these lords of commercialized virtue are spending, but the withheld wages of the American working class. . . . Health for China, a refuge for birds, food for the Belgians, pensions for New York widows, university training for the elite, and never a thought of a dollar for the thousands . . . who starved in Colorado."

In April, Walsh read the correspondence between
Rockefeller and CFI officers that he thought showed
Rockefeller lying that he knew little or nothing about
conditions in Colorado. He released the story to the
press and called Rockefeller back to explain. In this
hearing, Walsh accused Rockefeller of knowing about
specifics regarding poor work conditions, rents, scrip,
political corruption, and tactics used by security guards.
Rockefeller repeatedly denied it.

At one point Walsh put a photo before Rockefeller of
little Frank Snyder at the undertaker's after being shot
at Ludlow. "Do you care to look at it?" he asked.
Rockefeller replied, "You have described it, and I see
what the picture is." Rockefeller defended himself by
insisting that his letters and telegrams to the CFI officers
were supportive, not dictatorial; he let the officers in
Denver and the managers on location make the decisions.

The other IRC members thought Walsh was going too
far, but they could not stop him. When the final report
was turned in, several members objected to the "incendiary and revolutionary" tone they feared might worsen
relations between labor and capital. However, the IRC
had fulfilled its primary mission of gathering and evalu-
ating facts.

Rockefeller did not complain publicly about Walsh's
interviews. Guided by Mackenzie King, he came up with
a plan. Sometimes called the Industrial Representation
Plan, or simply the Rockefeller Plan, he presented it in
Pueblo, Colorado, on October 2, 1915. It allowed

employees to belong to a union but said they, not the union, would bargain with the managers. Every mine would elect at least two representatives who would meet annually with two company officials. The camps would be divided into five districts, with joint committees to meet four times yearly on health, sanitation, mine safety, recreation, and education. Check-weighmen would be elected, and periodic tours were mandated by the company president or his representative. Unsettled grievances could be appealed up to the company president. Discrimination against union members was forbidden. The mining camps would be open to union organizers.

The UMW rejected the plan. It was impossible, they said, for a worker to meet with the owner or his manager as an equal to work out a contract. They jeered the plan as a trick to restore Rockefeller's reputation. Employees were not equal to owners unless they had the force of an organized union behind them. But the miners voted for it overwhelmingly, 2,404 out of 2,846 ballots cast. The CFI officials voted for it unanimously.

On October 20, 1915, John D. Rockefeller Jr. began his tour of the eighteen CFI mines in the Trinidad field, where King had already been overseeing improvements. He saw the site of the former tent colony at Ludlow and the pit where the thirteen had died. He ate with the bachelor miners at the boardinghouses. He put on miners' clothing and went down into the mines. He inspected buildings, visited schools, and talked with the miners and their families. He and Mackenzie King even joined in the dancing with miners' wives. He was called "a mighty good mixer."

Rockefeller's new plan helped to begin a new tradition in American capitalism, but the price of these changes had been high. The strike in the Trinidad field was one of the longest in American labor history. It lasted 440 days, well over a year, during a harsh Colorado winter in which most of the strikers lived in tents after being driven from their homes. Twenty-four died during two days in April, and there were about a dozen lives lost during attacks in the time leading up to the strike. Mackenzie King's own research estimated that approximately two hundred died from both sides, including elderly people who died of pneumonia and other illnesses made worse by the exposure.

From a short-term perspective, the miners lost the strike. They did not get the union recognition that was their essential goal. However, the owners eventually lost the right to keep an open shop—their right to hire only nonunion workers or even require that their workers not belong to a union before being hired. The Wagner Act of 1935 upheld the closed shop, in which only union members may be hired. The Wagner Act was overturned by the 1947 Taft-Hartley Labor Act, however, and since 1951, states may individually choose between having union shops—in which workers must join the union after a certain period of time, in fairness to unions that have won prevailing wages and conditions—or a right-to-work law that supports the employer's right to hire nonunion workers.

There were other long-term consequences of the Colorado coalfield strike. Rockefeller's Industrial Representation Plan became a boon to the unionization movement. John Lawson recognized its significance when he said shortly after implementation, "I know they are going to recognize the union some time and this plan will prepare the way." When the plan or something similar was adopted by other companies, it began the process of teaching employers the benefit of regular contact with their employees and helped them get over their reflex fear of having union members in their workplace. As for the employees, the plan necessitated improvement of their organization and communication skills.

The effectiveness of federal troops in quieting the violence at Ludlow was a positive note for the future. In the Pullman Strike of 1894, when federal troops were sent in by President Cleveland without the request or knowledge of the governor of Illinois, they were accused of participating in the violence on the side of the owners. At Ludlow the troops were able to remain neutral. After the federal troops arrived, there were no more battles or killings, and miners, mine operators, and local communities wanted them to stay. Secretary of War Lindley Garrison said, "Injected in the midst of an inflamed populace, lately in open conflict, they restored and maintained order. Their poise, justness, absolute impartiality and effectiveness . . . commended them to all."

The granite monument to the Ludlow victims was desecrated by unknown vandals in 2003. The repaired monument was unveiled in June, 2005.

The various inquiries into the strike, both as it was ongoing and afterward, underlined the importance of investigatory commissions and committees. The Congressional Foster Committee and the Presidential Commission on Industrial Relations together produced several thousand pages of sworn testimony, as did the other investigations authorized by the governor of Colorado and the Colorado National Guard.

The Colorado coal miners took a stand for a principle—recognition of their union. Earlier famous American strikes, such as the McCormick Harvester Works Strike, the Homestead Strike, and the Pullman Strike, had been over wages and conditions. The primary goal of UMW District 15 miners was recognition of the union's right to bargain collectively with management; for this they fought and died, although the UMW national board gave up the goal late in the strike, before the Colorado miners were defeated. It was this principled stand that separates the Colorado coalfield strike from many of those that came before or after.

Today the mines of the Trinidad coalfields have long been closed. Oil, natural gas, new coalfields, and windmills have replaced them. Interstate 25 has eclipsed the railroads as traffic whips between Denver and Santa Fe. To the west, the Rockies rise in snow-capped majesty, and east of Ludlow, on the windswept plains, stands a granite monument erected by the United Mine Workers of America in 1918. The figures of a man, a woman, and a child stand at the base. On the rising column behind are chiseled these words:

In memory of
THE MEN, WOMEN AND CHILDREN,
WHO LOST THEIR LIVES
IN FREEDOM'S CAUSE
AT LUDLOW, COLORADO
APRIL 20, 1914.

TIMELINE

1913

July 24	United Mine Workers (UMW) organizer John Lawson announces goal of unionizing all coal miners in the state.
August	UMW Colorado District 15 secretary-treasurer Ed Doyle leases land, tents, and other supplies outside the camps for strikers when evicted.
August 26	Colorado Fuel & Iron (CFI) mine operators ignore two requests to meet with miners about their demands.
September 17	UMW leaders in Trinidad sign the call to strike.
September 23	Nine thousand miners strike and move out of company houses into tent colonies provided by UMW; at month's end, 11,000 of the 14,000 miners are on strike.
October 17	First appearance of Death Special armored car at Forbes tent colony; gunfire exchanged; one striker killed.
October 24	Three strikers killed in Walsenburg when CFI guards shoot into a crowd.
October 25-26	Skirmishing between miners and guards; in a blizzard, miners attack guards in several camps; guard John Nimmo is found shot to death in the snow.
October 28	Governor Elias Ammons signs executive order for Colorado National Guard troops to restore peace, with General John C. Chase in command.
October 30	President Woodrow Wilson requests officers of CFI to submit "a full and frank statement of reasons . . . to reject counsels of peace."
November 20	Baldwin-Felts security guard George Belcher gunned down in Trinidad by miner Louis Zancanelli.
November 26	U.S. labor secretary and Governor Ammons get miners and coal operators to work out an agreement; operators demand all miners vote; on November 30, the miners reject agreement without union recognition.

December 3-6	Blizzards create record snowfall of four to six feet. Drifts rise twelve to fifteen feet in the tent colonies, where 19,000 residents endure.
December 16	State Federation of Labor meets in Denver to discuss militia cruelty, intimidation, and the arrest of miners held without bail.
December 17	Mother Jones leads a protest march of 2,000 people to the state capitol building, denouncing Governor Ammons.

1914

January 4	Mother Jones arrested by General Chase in Trinidad and sent to Denver; on January 11, she escapes back to Trinidad and is put under military surveillance in San Rafael Hospital.
January 23	One thousand miners' wives and sympathizers march in solidarity for Mother Jones; General Chase falls off horse.
January 27	Congressman Edward Keating wins congressional investigation of the Colorado coalfields strike.
February 9	U.S. House Subcommittee on Mines and Mining, chaired by Congressman Martin Foster, begins hearings in the state capitol in Denver.
February 27	Governor Ammons withdraws all but two hundred Colorado militia from the strike zone due to huge expense.
March 10	General Chase orders militia to tear down tents in Forbes tent colony, where bloodhounds have tracked a trail from the crime scene.
April 6	John D. Rockefeller Jr. appears before the Foster Committee in Washington, DC, and supports the open shop as his basic principle.
April 14	Militia down to one company in strike zone; locals form a second company of mine guards, pit bosses, and vigilantes.
April 20	Shooting breaks out between militia and miners near Ludlow and turns into a gun battle; ten men (including Louis Tikas) and one child killed; about 5:30 PM, militia douse Ludlow colony tents with kerosene and set them afire; two women and eleven children die beneath a tent.
April 25	Sit-in at the capitol by Women's Peace Association to

demand federal troops; at 6:00 PM, Ammons wires President Wilson for help.

April 27   Funeral of Louis Tikas; several thousand march in silence.

April 30   Federal troops arrive in the strike zone; Colorado militia removed; ten-day war over.

May 27   U.S. Commission on Industrial Relations in New York City hears testimony.

August 1   John D. Rockefeller Jr. hires Canadian labor mediator Mackenzie King to help him better understand the place of unions in industrial relations.

September 5   President Wilson presents Fairley-Davies truce plan. Miners vote to accept; operators reject.

December 1   President Wilson appoints conciliation commission of three to end the strike; he scolds mine operators but cannot force them to give in.

December 7   Out of money to sustain strikers, defeated union leaders vote to end strike.

1915

January   Federal troops leave Colorado.

January 25   John D. Rockefeller Jr. testifies in New York City before the U.S. Commission on Industrial Relations, chaired by Missouri senator Frank Walsh.

April 21   John Lawson is tried and found guilty of the murder of John Nimmo; he is sentenced to life in prison.

September   With Mackenzie King, Rockefeller Jr. visits all CFI mines, talking to miners; they vote to accept his Industrial Representation Plan.

1916

June 21   Colorado Supreme Court declares invalid the 1914 election in mine camp precincts of Huerfano County; Sheriff Jeff Farr removed from office.

1917

April 20   Colorado Supreme Court ruling frees Lawson by reversing the district court conviction.

Sources

CHAPTER ONE: The Strike Scene
p. 10, "an exodus of woe . . ." Barron Beshoar, *Out of the Depths* (Denver, CO: Golden Bell, 1942), 63-64.

p. 10-11, "Every wagon was . . ." Ibid.

CHAPTER TWO: A Miner's Life
p. 25, "accident unavoidable . . . not timbering," George McGovern and Leonard Guttridge, *The Great Coalfield War* (Boston: Houghton Mifflin, 1972), 33.

p. 29, "very perfect political . . ." McGovern, *Great Coalfield War*, 29.

p. 29, "the kangaroo . . . down the canyon," Beshoar, *Out of the Depths*, 2.

p. 30, "ownership of courts . . ." McGovern, *Great Coalfield War*, 28.

CHAPTER THREE: The Rockefellers
p. 36, "common-sense business . . ." McGovern, *Great Coalfield War*, 9.

p. 42, "the well-being of . . ." *Columbia Encyclopedia*, 6th ed., s.v. "Rockefeller Foundation."

p. 44, "Soon the real . . ." Ron Chernow, *Titan* (New York: Random House, 1998), 574.

CHAPTER FOUR: United Mine Workers
p. 48, "An injury to one . . ." *Columbia Encyclopedia*, 6th ed., s.v. "Knights of Labor."

p. 49, "Labor produces . . ." McGovern, *Great Coalfield War*, 39.

p. 55, "not influenced . . ." Ibid., 82.

p. 56, "Joan of Arc . . ." Beshoar, *Out of the Depths*, 31.

p. 56, "Wherever there is . . . a hell-raiser," McGovern, *Great Coalfield War*, 100.

p. 56, "a fire-brand . . ." Ibid.

p. 59-60, "'Has anyone ever told you, my children . . ." Priscilla Long, *Mother Jones: Woman Organizer* (Cambridge, MA: Red Sun, 1976), 7-8.

CHAPTER FIVE: Demands

p. 61, "Labor is prior . . ." Roy Basler, ed. *Abraham Lincoln: His Speeches and Writings* (New York: Da Capo, 1946), 633-34.

p. 62, "This is the day . . ." Beshoar, *Out of the Depths*, 48.

p. 62,64, "If you are . . ." Ibid.

p. 68, "All right, you rat . . ." Ibid., 52.

p. 69, "a terrible unrest," McGovern, *Great Coalfield War*, 91.

CHAPTER SIX: Voice of the Gun

p. 72, "We will win . . ." George Korson, *Coal Dust on the Fiddle: Songs and Stories of the Bituminous Industry* (Hatboro, PA: Folklore Associates, 1965), 388-389.

p. 74, "There will be . . ." McGovern, *Great Coalfield War,* 109.

p. 74, "incendiary utterances," Ibid., 110.

p. 75, "Are you fellows . . ." Beshoar, *Out of the Depths*, 69.

p. 76, "Let every miner . . ." Ibid., 74.

p. 76, "The only language . . ." McGovern, *Great Coalfield War*, 119.

p. 76, "a strike of the . . ." Ibid., 112.

p. 77, "to drive the vicious . . ." Ibid., 121.

p. 78, "WE REPRESENT . . . ON TRIAL," Ibid., 123-24.

p. 80, "If you don't . . ." Ibid., 125.

p. 81, "looks hopeless . . . troops" Ibid., 133.

p. 82, "been made to . . ." Ibid., 134.

CHAPTER SEVEN: Martial Law

p. 85-86, "deeply disappointed . . . so critical," McGovern, *Great Coalfield War,* 135-36.

p. 86, "We will never . . ." Ibid.

p. 86, "Feudalism is no . . ." Ibid.

p. 87, "I care not . . ." Ibid., 146.

p. 87, "I can only . . ." Ibid., 147.

p. 88, "There is no . . ." Ibid., 156.

p. 89, "officers' shindigs," Ibid.

p. 90, "Sure, and I'm . . . your backsides," Beshoar, *Out of the Depths,* 110-111.

p. 93, "We have reason . . ." McGovern, *Great Coalfield War,* 168.

p. 93, "military surveillance," Ibid., 172.

p. 95, "GREAT CZAR FELL . . . " Ibid., 174.

p. 95, "General Chase . . ." Ibid., 175.

CHAPTER EIGHT: War

p. 98, "a restraining influence," McGovern, *Great Coalfield War,* 213.

p. 98, "the greatest single . . ." Ibid., 214.

p. 101, "men and soldiers . . ." Ibid., 224.

p. 102, "ceased to be an army . . ." Ibid., 227.

p. 102, "We've got Louie . . ." Ibid., 229.

p. 105, "horrible atrocities . . . to a finish," Ibid., 240.

p. 105, "For God's sake . . . constitutional rights," Ibid., 233.

p. 105, "to protect the . . ." Beshoar, *Out of the Depths,* 183.

p. 105-106, "We expect to break . . ." Ibid.

p. 107, "an industrial controversy . . ." McGovern, *Great Coalfield War,* 257.

CHAPTER NINE: Defeat

p. 113, "crimes were committed . . ." McGovern, *Great Coalfield War*, 288.

p. 114, "unfair to our workmen," Samuel Yellen, *American Labor Struggles*, (New York: SA Russel, 1936), 243.

p. 114, "No commission . . ." McGovern, *Great Coalfield War*, 306.

p. 115, "At least . . . create . . ." Ibid., 309.

p. 115, "We deem it the . . ." Ibid., 310.

p. 119, "safe for democracy," Woodrow Wilson, "Making the World 'Safe for Democracy,'" George Mason University, http://historymatters.gmu.edu/d/4943/ (accessed November 11, 2005).

CHAPTER TEN: Consequences

p. 123, "an impartial umpire," H. M. Gitelman, *Legacy of the Ludlow Massacre* (Philadelphia: University of Pennsylvania Press, 1988), 40.

p. 123, "My first impression . . ." Ibid., 46.

p. 123, "uncomplicated and well-intentioned," Ibid.

p. 124, "a new spirit abroad," Ibid., 64.

p. 124, "the task of . . ." McGovern, *Great Coalfield War*, 312.

p. 126, "I am more . . ." Ibid., 318.

p. 126, "I should think . . . my desire to," Ibid., 318-19.

p. 126-127, "It is not their . . ." Ibid., 320-21.

p. 128, "Do you care . . . the picture is," Ibid., 329.

p. 128, "incendiary and revolutionary," Ibid., 332.

p. 130, "a mighty good mixer," Ibid., 335.

p. 131, "I know they are . . ." Beshoar, *Out of the Depths*, 336.

p. 131, "Injected in the . . ." McGovern, *Great Coalfield War*, 310.

BIBLIOGRAPHY

Basler, Roy P., ed. *Abraham Lincoln: His Speeches and Writings.* New York: Da Capo Press Paperback, 1990 (unabridged republication of the edition published in 1946).

Beshoar, Barron B. *Out of the Depths: The Story of John R. Lawson, a Labor Leader.* Denver, CO: Golden Bell Press, 1942.

Chernow, Ron. *Titan.* New York: Random House, 1998.

The Columbia Encyclopedia. 6th ed. New York: Columbia University Press, 2000.

Dubofsky, Melvyn, and Foster Rhea Dulles. *Labor in America: A History.* 6th ed. Wheeling, IL: Harlan Davidson, 1999.

Filippelli, Ronald, ed. *Labor Conflict in the United States: An Encyclopedia.* New York: Garland Publishing, 1990.

Foner, Philip. *History of the Labor Movement in the United States.* Vol IV, *The Industrial Workers of the World, 1905-1917;* Vol. V, *The American Federation of Labor in the Progressive Era 1910-1915.* New York: International Publishers, 1980.

Gitelman, H. M. *Legacy of the Ludlow Massacre: A Chapter in American Industrial Relations.* Philadelphia: University of Pennsylvania Press, 1988.

Korson, George. *Coal Dust on the Fiddle: Songs and Stories of the Bituminous Industry.* Hatboro, PA: Folklore Associates, 1965.

Long, Priscilla. *Mother Jones: Woman Organizer: And Her Relations With Miners' Wives, Working Women, and the Suffrage Movement.* Cambridge, MA: Red Sun Press, 1976.

McGovern, George S., and Leonard Guttridge. *The Great Coalfield War.* Boston: Houghton Mifflin, 1972.

Yellen, Samuel. *American Labor Struggles.* New York: S. A. Russell, 1936.

WEB SITES

http://www.iww.org/en/node
The Industrial Workers of the World, a radical union, continues to advocate for the abolition of the wage system.

http://www.umwa.org
The United Mine Workers of America continues to advocate for the rights of workers. The home page contains a video of the rededication of the Ludlow Memorial in 2005.

http://www.rockfound.org
The Rockefeller Foundation continues to help underprivileged people around the world.

http://www.pbs.org/wgbh/amex/rockefellers/sfeature/sf_8.html
The PBS site related to the Ludlow Massacre, with many primary source quotations.

http://www.santafetrailscenicandhistoricbyway.org/ludlow.html
The Santa Fe Trail, a National Historic Trail, maintains a page about visiting the Ludlow Memorial and its history.

http://www.nlrb.gov/nlrb/home/default.asp
The National Labor Relations Board was created in 1935 and exists to oversee the interaction between private corporations and their employees and/or unions.

INDEX

American Federation of Labor (AFL), 49, 58, 61-62
Ammons, Elias, *66,* 66-67, 69, 77-79, 81-82, 83, 85-88, 92, 106-107, 108, 116
Anthracite coal strike, 46
Archbald, John D., 42

Baldwin-Felts Detective Agency, 50-51, 55, 68, *68,* 75, 81, 87, 96, 117, 119
Baltimore & Ohio (B & O) strike, 47
Belcher, George, 68, 77, 87, 117
Belk, Walter, 68, 77, 119
Bowers, LaMont, 37-38, 43, 55, 73, 76-77, 86-87, 97, 106, 120, 125
Brake, Edwin, 67, 69
Brown University, 40-41

Capp, MP, 55
Carlson, George, 116, *116,* 118
Carnegie Steel Company, 46
Chase, John, 79, 81-82, 83, *84,* 85, 87, 89-90, 92-97, 99-100, 103, 106, 113
Civil War, 15, 32, 46
Colorado Federation of Labor, 105-106
Colorado Fuel and Iron Company (CFI), 9, 19, 26-29, 35, 37-38, 43, 51-52, 65-66, 70, 73-74, 81, 85, 109-110, 113, 129
Costigan, Edward P., 29-30

Doyle, Ed, 62, 70, 90, 105, 112, 118, 125-126

Farr, Jefferson "King," 29, 55, 74, 118
Farrar, Fred, 116, 118
Foster, Martin D., 95, 125

Garrison, Lindley M., 131
Grisham, Jim, 74, 77, 79, 100

Hamrock, Patrick, 98-100, 103, 112
Harriman, Daisy, 56, 124
Hawkins, Horace, 64, 117
Hayes, Frank J., 62, 72, *73,* 74, 81, 90, 95, 112, 114-115, 118, 126
Haymarket Square riot, 48, *48*
Hendricks, John, 85
Hillyer, Granby, 116-117
Homestead Steel Strike, 31, 46, 133

Industrial Representation Plan (Rockefeller Plan), 128-131
International Workers of the World (IWW), 58, 62, 112, 121

Jones, Mary Harris "Mother," 56-60, *57,* 70, 74, 78, 86, 92-94, 96-97, 126

Kenehan, Roady, 79, 86, 89-90, 96
King, William Lyon Mackenzie,

121-125, *122,* 128-130
Knights of Labor, 48, 52, 57

Laurier, Wilfrid, 123
Lawson, John, 11-12, 52-56, *53,* 62, 69-70, 72, *73,* 75-76, 83-84, 90, 92-93, 99-100, 103, 105, 113, 117-119, 124-127, 131
Lincoln, Abraham, 61
Linderfelt, Karl, 79, *80,* 81, 89, 93, 97, 102, 104, 112-113, 117
Lippiatt, Gerald, 67-69, 87
Ludlow Massacre, *8, 10,* 89, *91, 100, 101, 104, 111*

McLennan, John, 62, 69
Mineowners' Association, 49
Missouri Pacific Railroad strike, 48

Nimmo, John, 81, 116-117

Osgood, John C., 34-37, *35*

Patterson, Thomas, 118
Peabody, James, 79
Pinkerton Detective Agency, 51
Progressive Movement, 47
Pullman, George, 36, 46
Pullman Strike, 46-47, 131, 133

Railroad uprisings of 1877, 46
Reno, William, 73-74
Robinson, Helen Ring, 107
Rockefeller, Abby Aldrich, 40
Rockefeller, Cettie, 39
Rockeller Foundation, 42-43, 121
Rockefeller, John D., 37-44,

38, 109, 120
Rockefeller, John D. Jr., 37, 39-44, *41,* 71, 76, 87, 89, 97, 106, 109-110, 112, 117-118, 120-126, 128-131
Roosevelt, Theodore, 46-47

Sherman Antitrust Act, 74, 78
Sinclair, Upton, 110
Snyder, Frank, 100, 105, 128
Standard Oil, 39-40
Stewart, Ethelbert, 76, 85-86

Taft, William Howard, 124
Taft-Hartley Labor Act, 130
Thomas, Mary Hannah, 72
Tikas, Louis, 93, 98-99, 102-104, 108, 113
Triangle Shirtwaist factory fire, 31-32

United Mine Workers (UMW), 9, 11, 49-52, 54-56, 58, 62-70, *63,* 72, 74, 76, 78, 89-90, 108, 112-115, 118-119, 129, 133

Van Cise, Philip, 83-84, 98

Walsh, Frank, 124-126, *127,* 128
Welborn, Jesse, 43, 55, 73, 89, 114, 120, 125
Western Federation of Miners (WFM), 49-50
Wilson, William, 87-88
Wilson, Woodrow, 47, 71, 85-87, *86,* 107, 108-110, 113-115, 119, 124

Zancanelli, Louis, 87, 117, 119